Using a Person-Centred Approach in Early Years Practice

Using a Person-Centred Approach in Early Years Practice reflects on the principles of person-centred counselling, developed by Carl Rogers. It guides students and practitioners to use this approach within the sphere of early childhood education, providing radical new ways of promoting emotions, emotional regulation and well-being.

This accessible resource reveals how a therapeutic approach with a humanistic perspective can be understood and woven into early years professional practice by practitioners themselves. Exploring how educators can be supportive through empathy, understanding and congruent in developing relationships, this text provides

- an overview and rationale to using a person-centred approach;
- its association to emotions, health and well-being;
- the role of therapeutic play in early years communities, from child, parents and wider team;
- how a person-centred approach can impact leadership and teamwork;
- its increasing necessity to supporting a child's physical and emotional development during the pandemic and beyond.

With informed practice examples, case studies and thought-provoking questions regarding a PCA, this book will be essential and informative reading for students studying early years or early childhood courses and to practitioners looking to improve and enhance their practice.

Amanda Norman is a Senior Lecturer and Programme Lead of the B.A. (Hons) Childhood Studies at the University of Winchester, UK.

T0384874

Using a Person-Centred Approach in Early Years Practice

A Therapeutic Guide for Students

Amanda Norman

Routledge
Taylor & Francis Group

LONDON AND NEW YORK

Designed cover image: © Getty Images

First published 2024
by Routledge
4 Park Square, Milton Park, Abingdon, Oxon OX14 4RN

and by Routledge
605 Third Avenue, New York, NY 10158

Routledge is an imprint of the Taylor & Francis Group,
an informa business

British Library Cataloguing-in-Publication Data
A catalogue record for this book is available from the British Library

Library of Congress Cataloging-in-Publication Data
Names: Norman, Amanda, author.
Title: Using a person-centred approach in early years practice and care :
a therapeutic guide for students / Amanda Norman.
Description: Abingdon, Oxon ; New York, NY : Routledge, 2024. |
Includes bibliographical references and index.
Identifiers: LCCN 2023011512 (print) | LCCN 2023011513 (ebook) |
ISBN 9781032224251 (hardback) | ISBN 9781032224244 (paperback) |
ISBN 9781003272526 (ebook)
Subjects: LCSH: Early childhood education--Psychological aspects. |
Emotions in children. | Student-centered learning.
Classification: LCC LB1139.23 .N66 2024 (print) |
LCC LB1139.23 (ebook) | DDC 372.2101/9--dc23/eng/20230426
LC record available at https://lccn.loc.gov/2023011512
LC ebook record available at https://lccn.loc.gov/2023011513

ISBN: 978-1-032-22425-1 (hbk)
ISBN: 978-1-032-22424-4 (pbk)
ISBN: 978-1-003-27252-6 (ebk)

DOI: 10.4324/9781003272526

Typeset in Optima
by KnowledgeWorks Global Ltd.

Contents

Contents

Introduction

This book explores a person-centred approach (PCA) in practice and focuses on its therapeutic value in both enhancing relationships and application within early years centres.

Rationale

This book contributes to a timely connection between the understanding and application of a person-centred approach (PCA) within early years. Developed within humanistic psychology, by Carl Rogers, in counselling and Virginia Axline with her work in child play therapy, a PCA will be explored in early years. This book is therefore intended to be read by those interested in supporting and understanding emotional development through play, within various early years centres. Early years centres defined within each chapter include formal day-care settings, nurseries, family centres, childminders and any other service offering early years care and education. The content of this book includes the principles of a therapeutic relationship and how these could be applied by professionals working with children under five years. It, therefore, aims to be a useful book resource, with informed practices included and case study examples provided about the complexities and appreciation of a PCA. These include reflections by the author and practice examples from her 30 years' experience of working with children, their families and professionals within and beyond the local community.

This book aims to illuminate how a PCA could be central to early years practice. Research, theory and practice are included within each chapter to support and strengthen the value of working within a PCA although is not intended as a one-size-fits-all approach. Rather this book's aim is to be an interactive guide to the way practitioners can reflect and extend their professional practice with the children and adults they care and work with.

This book will be a valuable and timely contribution to the field of early years because it aims to discuss therapeutic approaches without proposing practitioners become therapists. Rather it is about how informed practices can lead to deeper reflections and thinking about the way children's emotions could be supported. Young children's transitional spaces and consistent

DOI: 10.4324/9781003272526-1

primary carers, either from their home or childcare setting, have been disrupted because of lockdown. A wider knowledge of emotional understanding about young children is therefore increasingly important with young children having experienced living in a pandemic and this book serves to bridge the work of Rogers and Axline's principles, as a humanistic psychological perspective, within contemporary early years practice (Axline, 1974).

In studying the history of a PCA, it leads into a discussion about the theory and then practice and thinking about a PCA today. Attention to how a PCA can be an inclusive approach, particularly pertinent to the current climate surrounding COVID and returning to settings, is also discussed within the latter chapters.

Presenting multiple perspectives, drawing on history, education, health, welfare, sociology and social policy as a way of considering how a PCA underpins understandings of babies and young children, and childhood is included. It also enables students to understand and analyse the processes and arc of a PCA that can shape childhood and children's lives in a way that fosters critical evaluation, and which includes an understanding of the contested and changing nature of the concept of childhood, ethical principles and children's rights.

What This Book Is Not

The overall intention of this book is an opportunity to embrace and implement informed features of a PCA in early years practice, from conception to four years of age, assimilating and appreciating the therapeutic approaches that could valuable to practice. In reviewing a PCA, this book explores, describes, analyses and evaluates both counselling and therapeutic approaches but does not seek to underplay or imply that by employing these approaches qualifies an individual to be a counsellor, psychotherapist or play therapist. These are specialist professions with specific training and understanding about client-therapist relationships. Instead, this book seeks to explore the therapeutic approaches and the principles of a PCA as a way of enhancing communication, supporting emotions, connection and relationships with both parents, practitioners and children within an education and care contexts. To fully appreciate the PCA, an exploration into its origins and humanistic psychological paradigm will initially be discussed (Rogers, 1980).

Connections to Other Professions

Connected to current theories and approaches towards personal, social and emotional learning and development will then lead to an insight of a PCA within contemporary early years centres. This will be developed with reference to how the pandemic has created opportunities for reflection and considered ways of connecting to other professions including psychologists, counsellors and the nursing profession.

Contextualised Reflections and COVID

Predominately this book is geographically situated within England and Europe, although examples have also been included beyond the West. The reader may have an interest in working within educational, social, health or care contexts with young children. There is often a focus and interest towards the older child and education more broadly in studying early years, with topics including readiness for formal schooling, policy and practices when studying early years. The aim for this book is to further contribute to the early years field with an extension towards supporting self-regulation with children and creating a nurturing early years community. This book, therefore, is recommended as an educational as well as a general resource for those wanting to understand more about the origins of PCA and adopting it as a whole setting approach.

In recent years, the regular caring of infants and young children has been increasingly sought within and beyond the home, with many parents in the west seeking professional care as they return to employment or opt to share their childcare (Tickell, 2011). It is also, therefore, considered a judicious addition to understand and value the context of various relationships and care between infants, parents and professionals.

A broad range of themes included in this book navigates the reader towards specialist subjects and concepts. Care and tuned-in relationships are key to early childhood education and yet therapeutic approaches to support emotions are often predominately left to external experts or for those undertaking specific training in addition to their early years qualifications achieved. This book guides practitioners through the potentials of understanding an approach that brings the early years community together and provides ways of promoting and supporting emotions, self-regulation and well-being through a PCA. It, therefore, examines young children's emotional states connected to PCA. It reveals how a therapeutic approach and process within a humanistic perspective can be understood and weaved within early years professional practice. It also highlights how the approach can facilitate and enrich and environment to include experiences for individual children and educators that focus and support their emotional well-being. This book explores how educators can be supportive through empathy, understanding and congruent in developing relationships.

This book covers a wide scope of topics related to a PCA.

- An overview and rationale to using a PCA
- A PCA and association to emotions, health and well-being
- A PCA in early years practice and therapeutic play
- A PCA in supporting the early years setting community, from the child, parents to the team
- A PCA to leadership and teamwork through supervision and beyond
- A PCA in creating a thriving and inclusive environment

Chapter 1 Person-Centred Principles: A Rogerian Approach and Principles

This chapter outlines the rationale for writing about a PCA and contextualises the historical and contemporary applications.

The PCA is viewed as a set of values, skills and tools used in getting to know someone, what they find important and what they want out of life. Beyond counselling, where person-centred therapy historically resides, a PCA can be thought of as a philosophy, a way of thinking or a mindset which involves viewing, listening to and supporting a person or child, based on their strengths, abilities, aspirations and preferences regarding the decisions to developing and maintaining meaning in their life. A PCA way of thinking are therefore the basis for action in all kinds of situations, from planning, to organisation, and understanding and connecting with communities.

As an approach within early years context, it is a humanistic way of working, interested in the intrinsic motivations of the individual.

Chapter 2 Person-Centred Practice: Therapeutic Play in Early Years Practice

Therapeutic play and its relevance to creativity, autonomy and self-esteem are discussed with the principles of a PCA in a non-judgemental, open and honest way. Through communication and play, children are selecting how much they openly share with others. Within a relaxed, present, engaged and non-judgemental carer, more is shared, communicated and known about each other and about themselves. The therapeutic principles themselves make common sense to those working in the early years, offering environments that are welcoming, engaging, safe, secure and open to all. This enables opportunities for open honesty and healthy attachments. Play is always a creative act in which people develop narratives, imagine and explore the world. In therapeutic play, the child is given the opportunity to explore without limitations or everyday boundaries.

Chapter 3 Person-Centred Care: Supporting Emotions with Young Children

This chapter examines a PCA and the way it can support the emotions of the young child. It includes the value of a PCA and the links to the EYFS (21) curriculum, attachment, and emotional literacy theory. It also includes a discussion about the uniqueness of the child and their rights in early years context.

Within the context of childcare settings being overshadowed by the pandemic young children and their emotions will be explored in relation to their mental health and well-being, with a call for further attention to develop and implement innovative strategies. A PCA promotes a caring culture through practical and shared strategies that have meaning for those with varying child development knowledge and experience. It will be these areas that will form the focus of this chapter.

Chapter 4 Person-Centred Support: Supervision in Early Years Practice

This chapter focuses on the value of a PCA during supervision and in planning and supporting a practitioner's development. Person-centred supervision and planning emphasises the importance of learning from observation and the intrinsic motivation. This can be applied at differing levels to both leaders and practitioners in their roles.

Chapter 5 Person-Centred Thinking and Listening: Parent Partnership in Early Years Practise

PCA is a humanistic way of working and looks at the intrinsic motivations of the individual. As practitioners, the following three core elements navigate the parent relationship and will be the core thread of the chapter:

- Understanding – of a given situation and mindset
- Congruence – being open and honest in communication
- Empathy – not getting embroiled in emotions but appreciating situations and the emotions attached to them (Rogers, 1980).

This chapter focuses on the PCA as way of discovering and acting on what is important to a person and what is important for them.

Chapter 6 Person-Centred Planning: Teamwork and Leadership in Early Years Practise

As a teacher of adults, the PCA recognises the potential in others rather than imposing a model to conform to. By engaging in varied job roles with colleagues, parents and infants, I have managed to apply Roger's work to my professional relationships. Throughout this chapter, I will include examples about the way congruence was developed within the team, the authentic self-revealed and the acceptance, personal thoughts, and feelings that may correspond or differ to others.

Chapter 7 Person-Centred Approach: An Inclusive Approach

A PCA places the child and their family at the centre. This way of working reflects what a child can do, what is important to them (now and in the future) and thinks about what support they might need to reach their potential. It is a continuous process of listening, learning and action to support the child and their family to get what they want out of life. Applying a PCA includes problem solving and thinking about how the most appropriate support and resources are accessed to enable children to work towards their aspirations. It is a way of thinking and relating to the world and other people rather than a specific technique, tool or strategy.

A Model of Practice: Person-Centred Early Education Practice

Each chapter will focus on an aspect of the model proposed and this will be a way of linking the practice to theory throughout this book. The model encompasses the three core conditions that Rogers considers essential to person-centred relationships. Within this, I have then considered how this could include elements of practice.

Leading and learning: Learning from the children, their parents as well as from experienced practitioners internally and externally as part of an early years community.

Respectful relationships with families: This element focused on how parent relationships are introduced, developed, navigated and fluid within the early years community.

Holistic play: This considers and reflects the value of play in all its forms and the adult's role within this play relationship. It considers the principles of play therapy and how aspects could be aligned to play when engaged in early years communities.

Caring communities: This focuses on caring within and beyond the early years community. It includes thinking about the value of supervision and inclusive practice within a PCA.

This focuses on how teams and leadership can work through a PCA and develop a positive and thriving early years community so that the children observe the practitioners valuing and respecting each other.

As a starting point, Person-Centred Early Education Practice (PEEP) model has been designed as an infographic, visual aid, to be shared as a way of developing a PCA into early years practice at a community level. Each chapter includes an element from the PEEP model (Fig. 0.1).

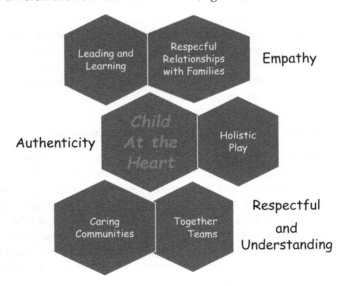

Figure 0.1 Person-centred early education practice (PEEP)

Activities and Practice Links

Within each chapter, a Toolkit for Practice will also offer ideas for practice and how some of the themes presented could be reflected and shared as a community within their local early years centres. Rather than a technique, the practices included are illustrative examples of approaching PCA within a particular early years centre. These are to develop reflective thinking about how a person-centred approach could be considered as a purposeful thread of practice when engaging with each other. Practitioners as a community, with leaders and families as well as the children, may reflect and decide how it could be weaved into their everyday practice that is relevant to them and their local culture.

A process of planning preparation and self-reflection is central to transformative practice. Being active on this journey is therefore key to creating a successful person-centred early years centre. The focused questions and pictures of practice alongside the toolkit are all included as prompts to support the journey.

Keywords

- Attachment
- Person centred
- Teamwork
- Supervision
- Play
- Care
- Empathy

References

Axline, V. M. (1974) *Play Therapy*. New York, NY: Ballantine Books.

Rogers, C. R. (1980) *A Way of Being*. Boston, MA: Houghton-Mifflin.

Tickell, C. (2011) *The Early Years: Foundations for Life, Health and Learning*. www.gov.uk/government/uploads/system/uploads/attachment_data/file/180919/DFE-00177-2011.pdf (Accessed 15 Nov 2021).

1   Person-Centred Principles

A Rogerian approach and principles

Introduction

This chapter introduces the overarching principles of a person-centred approach (PCA) with specific reference to its founder, Carl Rogers (1981), from the mid-twentieth century. It will include a historical overview about person centredness, with specific reference to how it was developed in England. Initially, the theory of PCA will be explored to gain an appreciation to the philosophical ways of working with others and thinking about practice more generally (Lyon and Rogers, 1981). It will therefore include how person centredness has been used therapeutically between clients and counsellors. Focus of the therapeutic self and relevant meanings will then shape how this could be extended to relationships beyond a specific and disciplined therapeutic relationship to that of counsellor and client. By making connections and contextualising the PCA, aligned philosophical and pedagogical positions in early years will be included. Therapeutic threads of thinking about a PCA will conclude the chapter.

Defining and Exploring a Person-Centred Approach

In understanding a PCA, this journey begins with an introduction to the theory and consideration of its relevance. Although PCA is the term consistently referred to it does not seek to diminish person centredness as a superficial and limiting approach, with a one size fits all and something we 'do'. I think it is much more than that. It is concerned with reflection and consideration to the philosophical ways of thinking about how we engage, where we position ourselves in relationships and why this occurs.

As an educationalist, I view person centredness within a PCA to be a relational and compassionate care pedagogy. It encourages the slowing and development of meaningful interactions within the fast-paced macro- and micro-societies, both children and adults live (Fig. 1.1). It could be considered, in part, a contemplative pedagogy, and the purpose of this chapter is for the reader to develop connections and meanings for themselves in

DOI: 10.4324/9781003272526-2

Figure 1.1 The journey is as valuable as the destination

understanding more about a PCA. In the subsequent chapters, the exploration and examination of person centeredness creates a space for practitioners to reflect, explore and question, with curiosity how their practice with the children in their care and as a team could be re-evaluated, shaped and developed.

Connecting Principles with Everyday Practice

In developing a PCA, a model for practice has been created as a visual way that could be developed as part of working within a PCA (Fig. 1.2). Each subsequent chapter will highlight an element outlined but all aims to place the **child at the heart** of the PCA.

This chapter discusses three areas: **authenticity, respectful and understanding and empathy** in the practice model proposed.

Figure 1.2 Person-centred early education practice (PEEP)

The core aspects that underpin a PCA are through these three guiding principles and often defined as

- Congruence: This term is about authenticity, genuineness and honesty within relationships.
- Empathy: This is the ability to feel what others feel when interacting in the moment-to-moment interactions as they occur.
- Respect and understanding (unconditional positive regard): This principle is concerned with the acceptance, unconditional positive regard towards the client, as defined by Rogers but can be widened to include the individual, child and/or adult (Rogers, 1951).

This chapter introduces and outlines how these three principles are applied in a counselling relationship and how the principles of a PCA have been a thread throughout history when considering early years' pioneers and theorists.

Connections in Understanding Individuals Thinking and Understanding within a PCA

Humanistic psychology is considered a psychological perspective and was often considered a response to the dominant mid-twentieth century psychoanalytic theory and behaviourism of the time to how development was understood and supported. Philosophies of realism and positivism informed much of the research with children, underpinned by a quantitative/scientific approach. The humanistic approach, humanistic therapy was derived from the work of philosophers such as Heidegger and Satire and their existential and phenomenology thinking. Existentialism emphasises the existence of an individual person as a free and responsible agent who can determine their own development though acts of will. Human beings are basically good, altruistic and strive towards goodness if they are given the opportunity. Phenomenology, developed by Husserl, asserts that there is no one single reality. Reality is instead a construct of the individual experience (Dryden and Reeves, 2013). It is the subjective experience of the client that is important and the only meanings that should be attached to that experience are those that the person experiences rather than the interpretations of others. Individuals within the humanistic perspective are considered to have the ability to know how to self-heal and are capable of self-direction, given the opportunity to explore and space to do this, with nurturing individuals around them. In a PCA theory, it connects closely to how we view the child–practitioner relationship. It proposes that the individual (the child) should be trusted to find their own way forward and that the role of the counsellor (the practitioner, in early years) is one of the companions which can encourage a relationship, so they feel safe to experience their own experiences.

Humanistic psychology became popular in the 1960s when the cultural emphasis was on emancipation from traditional values and beliefs (Bekerian and Levey, 2002). It was an alternative exploration of new ideas and attitudes both personally and politically. Although humanistic psychologists did not entirely discard the idea of scientific psychology and of psychoanalysis, a move beyond them was timely with increased inspiration from a variety of sources including European philosophy. Wider interest and knowledge about alternative practices on the mind and body, within cultures beyond Europe was also considered a valuable contribution to shifts in thinking about how people behave and think (Phoenix and Thomas, 2002).

A Person-Centred Approach and Mindfulness

Mindfulness is increasingly used in schools and early years' settings alongside other practices such as yoga, so how different are they to a PCA?

Mindfulness relates to Buddhist practice, the concept of observing one's own thoughts and actions and reflecting on the present moment in daily life. It is about developing kind and honest speech patterns akin to PCA. Carl Rogers describes psychological growth as occurring from supportive conditions that enable the positive direction towards being at one with themselves. Although mindfulness is practised within the self rather than with a facilitator or therapist relationship, it also encourages a non-judgemental attitude towards oneself, honesty and an attitude of self-compassion. Similarly, person centredness was connected to unconditional positive regard, congruence and empathy.

Focused Question

Do you practice mindfulness or any other activities that help you to relax and have space for yourself?

If you do practice any form of self-care activities, consider how they are connected with a PCA?

If you do not practice or spend any time on yourself, consider what you could do that evokes a sense of self-compassion and kindness for yourself.

After all to care for others, you also need to care for yourself.... (Clare, 2018: 12) (Fig. 1.3).

Humanistic psychology was often referred to as the 'third force' in psychology. In phenomenological research, the lived experience of human beings is the ultimate source of all meaning and value. Phenomenology, a philosophical approach to human nature, began in Europe with Edmund Husserl (1859–1938), emphasising that the subjective experience of the

Figure 1.3 Mindfulness and yoga in the early years

individual awareness (what they hear, sense, feel) is everything (Phoenix and Thomas, 2002). The immediate, conscious experience, interpreted by the person is considered significant and is concerned with the here and now. Therefore, human psychology is referred to the way that each of us is intrinsically involved in the process of existence. It is concerned with being a distinct individual immersed in the flow of experience as they move through lifespan. This approach agrees that in most situations, individuals are aware of having some autonomy and a sense of empowerment with the ability to make choices. The power of choice in action allows the opportunity for a person to decide who they would like to become. It is a process referred to as personal growth. Like psychoanalysis, humanistic psychologists are concerned with supporting individual through their desired change as they experience it. The focus for them relates to an understanding of feelings in themselves and exploring alternatives. It generally takes a holistic approach and at the core of the experience is the flow of conscious awareness. Conscious experience is structured into meaningful patterns which are embedded in a reality. Much of the time, a person can navigate and infer a measured coherence and interconnectedness of the predictability of events. However, occasional reflections may occur with experiences such as a bereavement or birth that can alert us to the existence of the unknown, revealing what we do not know within the life we experience, an 'aha', self-aware of our possibilities and limitations, moment. Tragedies or even intoxications may also significantly alter an individual's conscious state. These may be defined as peak experiences and are types of conscious self-awareness. The influential humanistic psychologist Abraham Maslow (1973 in Maslow, 2022) termed peak experiences as being characterised by a sudden shift in consciousness as they experience the shift from perhaps a cataclysmic event or momentary experience that occurred. Maslow's research indicated that peak experiences are ignited in a variety of situations (Maslow, 2022). These can be from mundane experiences from sitting with family and having a meal or walking home after having studied intensely for several hours to those more significant moments in life such as a tragedy occurring (Maslow, 1962). The peak experience of the moment has its own intrinsic meaning and wholeness and is therefore a sense of fusion with life. Anxiety is completely absent during this peak experience.

Rogers believes that psychologically healthy individuals as adults are open to experience without feeling threatened and can listen to themselves and others. They are aware of their feelings and the feelings of others. They have the capacity to live in the present moment and they trust their decisions instead of searching for guidance from others. Rogers considers the ability of individuals in being able to hold their source of wisdom within themselves, having an internal locus of evaluation. A PCA proposes that everyone holds within themselves the capacity to grow towards the fulfilment of their unique selves, to reach their peak experience. In considering Abraham Maslow (1973 in Maslow, 2022), a humanistic theorist, and his hierarchy of needs, he

---

Maslow's Hierarchy of Needs
Self-actualisation
(Achieving your full potential)
Self-esteem
(Accomplishment)
Love/belonging
(Relationships and friends)
Safety
(security)
Physical needs
(Food, water, and rest)

Figure 1.4 Maslow's hierarchy of needs self-actualisation

proposed that behaviour arises from the way in which we continually strive to satisfy our various needs, from physical needs to how we manage our self-esteem needs. Maslow summarised needs as being physical, psychological safety, esteem and self-actualisation. His theory includes how an individual is motivated to meet these needs but also the desire to maintain them. These needs arise in an invariant sequence of urgency, represented hierarchically, and suggest that a person is constantly motivated to satisfy their differing needs, as each need is fulfilled (Fig. 1.4).

The ultimate point is that of self-actualisation. Self-actualisation is the fulfilment of one's highest personal potential with the other needs below. It can take many forms but basically is about a person becoming more truly themselves. Maslow's work is particularly interesting because unlike some other theories, he chose to study not those who are psychologically unwell but those with the human potential and those that had achieved their potential. A person experiencing self-actualisation, as Rogers concurs, is when a person can become so engaged in the present moment that all the other matters in life disappear and they are completely invested in that moment, free from the constraints of anxiety.

A PCA in counselling does not encourage techniques or fixes but focuses on the therapeutic relationship. Areas including reflection summarising and paraphrasing are important. These areas can assist the client to relax to identify their feelings and to express themselves by feeling listened to, as well as listening for, any inconsistencies and feelings which can be explored later. Rogers proposes a therapeutic process that supports the process of moving towards self-actualisation. He proposed seven stages, beginning at one, which in the right environment, potentiality unfolds self-actualisation.

1   Cannot speak openly about feelings and is not able to take responsibility for his pain but will instead blame others; it is unlikely that clients arrive at counselling willingly at this stage.
2   Client experiencing less rigidity with a small movement was wondering whether some responsibility should be taken.

3 Client considers taking more responsibility but tends to generalise and put more focus on the path and present feelings; this can be a common stage to enter therapy.
4 Client is more in touch with their present feelings and tends to be critical towards themselves.
5 Client is more connected with current feelings and can experience and express them.
6 Client has realisation of previously being stuck and now recognises their own processes. This is the work towards self-actualisation feeling more empathy towards self and others.
7 Clients' conditions of worth are replaced by internally generated fields and become a fluid self-accepting person who is open to the changes that life presents (Kelly, 2017: 72; Rogers, 1961).

While this book is concerned with a PCA beyond the counselling relationship, having an understanding about the process of the client, counsellor relationship can gain an appreciation to the way therapeutic relationships can be formed and developed in many areas of professional lives when engaging with others and reflecting on ourselves. Certainly, in some aspects of my professional and personal life, I have had moments of what I could define as small epiphanies, or at one in the moment of something I was immersed in doing, such as writing or painting and even singing a good night song to my daughter and son, which could be interpreted as self-actualising.

Maslow (1962) believed that peak experiences have the potential to stimulate individuals to reflect on their own experience and the potential, available possibilities before them. Flow experience is personal and the complete involvement in an activity experience is enjoyed for its own sake. A further assumption within humanistic psychology is that individuals are basically good and have an innate need to make themselves and the world better (Hoffman, 1994). The humanistic perspective therefore moved away from making generalisations, with the focus on the personal worth of the individual. This includes the centrality of human values, and the creative, active nature of human beings. Humanistic psychology is optimistic in the human capacity to overcome hardship, pain and despair. Central to the practice of humanistic psychology is a PCA (Phoenix and Thomas, 2002).

A Growing Trend in Britain

As an explicit movement in the late 1950s, humanistic psychology was popularised by psychologists Abraham Maslow, George Kelly, Carl Rogers and Gordon Alport. While there is not a singular dominated figure in human psychology, Carl Rogers was perhaps considered the closest (Bekerian and Levey, 2002).

In Britain, the influence of Carl Rogers (Sanders, 2021) significantly grew, and this was initially within marriage guidance counselling. In the 1960s, his PCA to counselling was disseminated and studied in British universities and within school counselling training courses. As discussed, Carl Rogers defines a fully functioning person as being able to seek out new experiences physically and psychologically, as well as mastering new skills. The quality of the fully functioning person has an ability to be open to experience existential living, trust, creativity and autonomous decision-making. It also includes the ability to experience freedom. From childhood to adulthood, positive regard was regarded as key to personal growth. Positive regard is the affection, approval and acceptance needed from the important people in children's lives (particularly parents), unconditionally. Having positive self-regard influences and enhances self-esteem, self-worth and positive self-image. This is enhanced through interactions which are

- Congruent: genuineness, honesty with the client.
- Empathic: the ability to feel what the client feels.
- Respectful and understood: acceptance, an unconditional positive regard towards the client (Corey, 1996: 202).

Carl Rogers, the Person

In understanding a PCA more thoroughly, Carl Roger's own life story is helpful in appreciating the timeline. He was born in rural Illinois, USA, in 1902 and was a quiet and shy child. He went to university to study agriculture, then Christianity. After marrying his childhood friend Helen Elliott, he studied psychology at the Teachers College, Columbia University. He then worked with children and their families for 12 years in Rochester, New York, and during this time began to develop his own ideas about the individuals and self-healing (Thorne, 2013 in Dryden and Reeves, 2013).

Rogers then took up an appointment in 1928 as a member of the child study department of the society for the prevention of cruelty to children in Rochester New York, USA. He joined an institution where the three fields of psychology psychiatry and social work were combining forces in diagnosing and treating problems; these contacts appealed to Rogers' essentially pragmatic temperament. By 1940, Rogers was a professor of psychology at Ohio State University and his first book counselling and psychotherapy appeared two years later from 1945 to 1957; he was professor of psychology at Chicago a period of intense activity much research carried out on person-centred therapy publication of client-centred therapy in 1951 (Thorne 2013: 121 in Dryden and Reeves, 2013).

As a therapist he considered the client–therapist relationship as co-working together rather than the counsellor as expert in the healing process. He continued to develop his theories in 1950s and was particularly concerned to validate his ideas through research, making a huge contribution to research in psychotherapy. Throughout his life, he inspired many projects in the 1960s, 1970s and 1980s to evaluate the effectiveness of counselling and psychotherapy. He continued to broaden his vision beyond counselling psychotherapy to relationships in education and politics until his death in 1987 (Merry, 1999; Sanders, 2021).

A Rogerian Counselling Relationship: A Person-Centred Approach within the Clinical Therapeutic Relationship

In understanding a PCA landscape, understanding and reflecting about how Rogers intended it to be an active counselling relationship is relevant to the discussion.

The therapist within a PCA does not focus on problems and solutions but on the whole person in the relationship. They invest themselves freely and fully in their relationship with the clients. The idea is that they gain entrance into the world of the client as an emotional commitment. The therapist is willing to involve themselves alongside the client they are working with. The intention is not for an all-knowing therapist, distant from the client because the goal is for clients to become a fully functioning person with good psychological health. It is therefore an invested relationship, with the aim being that the client moves away from the facades of living up to the expectations of others, including the therapist. The intention is towards valuing honesty and the capacity of accepting and evaluating oneself and one's own feelings. Respect and understanding of others and nurturing close relationships with a willing to risk being open to all in everyday experiences (Tolan, 2003; Sanders, 2021).

The client–therapist relationship from a PCA is to create positions of growth and enabling a capacity to grow towards a fulfilment of their unique identity. Often self-concepts can be blocked or distorted where the person has had relationships, whereby they have been negatively perceived (Mearns et al., 2013). The therapist's task is to create new conditions or relationships for further growth processes that can be encouraged, modified and transformed. Rogers believes that three core conditions are essential for this to occur. The first element is on the realness or genuineness or congruence of the therapist. The more the therapist can be himself in the relationship without putting up a professional front or a personal facade, the greater will be the chance of the client changing developing into a positive constructive manner. The therapist who is honest and congruent, conveys the message that is not only permissible but also desirable to be himself. They should have the ability to offer the client a total acceptance of unconditional positive regard. The client is then able to embrace his attitude of acceptance and non-judgementalism (Merry, 1999). The therapeutic movement is much more likely when the client can feel safe and to explore negative feelings moving into the core of his anxiety. It is more likely to sense the first momentary feelings of self-acceptance. The third element of the therapeutic relationship is empathic understanding and within this is the capacity to track and sense the feelings and personal meanings of the client (Rogers, 1961).

Rogers (1961) wrote extensively about empathy and of the three core conditions was considered a principle that could be learnt. For him it was essential to be empathic as well as being understanding. To appreciate the client's perceptual, subjective world with sensitivity to the moment-to-moment experiencing is important because they are wanting to be recognised as a reliable companion (McCormack and McCance, 2016). Empathy can occur even when the therapist may be experiencing a contradictory feeling to that of the client, being able to move into someone's else's inner world without the fear of being overwhelmed by it.

Rogers (1975) considered therapeutic relationships moved through three distinct phases:

- The first stage is characterised by the establishment of trust and may happen very rapidly or take months.
- The second stage sees the development of intimacy during the stage the client is enabled to reveal some of the people's levels of his or her experiencing.
- The third stage is characterised by an increasing utility mutuality between therapist and client when such a stage is reached, likely the client (and therapist) will be increasingly self-disclosing and will be challenged to risk more of themselves in the relationship (Rogers, 1961, 1983).

This three-stage process increases relationships to become rewarding, and culminating in achieving a mutuality deep PCA, with questions about the process and reflections (Mearns et al., 2013: 138). A person who is cared about begins to feel at a deep level that perhaps they are after all worth being cared for. While early years' practitioners would not be practising therapy, the therapeutic relationship is helpful in exploring and evaluating ways a PCA could be approached in early years.

Beyond a Rogerian Approach in Counselling: A Therapeutic Approach but Not Application of Therapy in Education

In my previous role as therapeutic play specialist one of the concerns by educators and myself was encouraging those who were not a specialist in counselling or play therapy to practice and diagnose children and their needs. There are professionals with specific training in play to support children's individual needs. In working with children every day in care and educational contexts, a therapeutic approach is not about implementing therapy but considering how children's and adults personal, emotional and social needs within and beyond an educational curriculum could be met.

Judith Horvath (2021), a manager at Olympus KeyMed Day Nursery in Southend, Essex, wrote that play is a language that can have considerable therapeutic benefits. As she highlights play therapy, principles are aligned to early years' practitioners in many ways.

Virginia Axline (1974) stated that adults should

- Develop a warm and friendly relationship with the child
- Accept the child as they are not what they should or could be
- Establish a feeling of permission in the relationship so that the child feels free to express their feelings completely

- Be alert to the feelings the child is expressing and reflect these feelings back in such a manner that the child gains insight into their behaviour
- Maintain a deep respect for the child's own ability in finding solutions to problems as occur, and giving the child the time and opportunity to do so
- Avoid attempting to direct the child's actions or conversations in any manner as the child leads the way
- Avoid hurrying the time along as play is a gradual process, with many facets
- Only establish those limitations necessary to anchor the time to the world of reality and to make the child aware of his or her responsibility in the situation (Axline, 1974; Horvath and Symonds. 1991)

However, Horvath (2021) also highlighted that it is important to recognise the difference between the therapeutic benefits of play for all children and the use of play therapy for the 20 per cent of the UK's children who suffer from a social, behaviour, emotional or mental health problem. There are risks in using play for therapeutic purposes without training and clinical supervision. Therefore, a PCA and child-centred approach (CCA) includes a framework to think about emotional relationships and play in areas such meeting emotional and social needs, space to communicate together and work creatively together to support wellbeing (Horvath, 2021). Children need unconditional acceptance to grow a healthy self-concept, and this can be achieved by supporting and co-regulating the child's feelings. Conditional positive regard and loved for being themselves is at the heart of a PCA and in counselling relationships, Rogers would put individuals at the heart of the experience. He would focus on being there as a companion, facilitator within the clients self-healing potential of the change process rather than the often-professional psychological expert in dealing with behaviour (Merry, 1999; Tolan, 2003). For him individuals can move towards their true potential in a constructed way and be fully functioning. By developing a way of trying to understand individual's inner world in co-regulation, it promotes a more genuine approach, then the expert identifying the problems of an individual. In working with staff at a nursery, I noted what the PCA could offer, reflecting on my own experiences and by engaging in a PCA, it provided me with a theoretical understanding and practice to how communication including listening can be so powerful in daily interactions. PCA was a journey about working with colleagues, parents and children.

A PCA and Its Connections and Relevance to Early Years Care

According to Smith (2013 in McCormack and McCance, 2016), the values and core conditions of a child-centred context emerge with three core conditions. These are, as already discussed,

- congruence
- unconditional positive regard
- empathic understanding of their internal frame of reference

Being valued as an equal to the therapist in the relationship is at the heart of a Rogerian approach. Maintaining a similar physical level encourages relational body language that offers good eye contact between the two creating safe spaces and offering relationships that are respectful and meet clients in their level without patronising genuineness remarks that are insincere (McCormack and McCance, 2016).

Unconditional positive regard is about reducing assumptions of judgements in creating positive and accepting attitudes towards the child. Change is more likely to occur when the practitioner is therefore willing to be emotionally engaged with the children, with empathy honesty and unconditional positive regard. Empathic understanding experienced it and communicated in accepting the child for who they are, they in turn can become more nurturing themselves; they feel really listened to and more attentive to their inner experiences (Rogers, 1980: 117).

As PCA is not a repertoire of techniques, but it is rather a person's system of underpinning values and an integrated aspect of that person a continual process.

Focused Question

Can you reflect and write an experience where you as a professional felt you had supported a child

- *by being congruent with them*
- *providing unconditional positive regard*
- *having an empathic understanding*

Are there times where you felt one or all these areas could have been considered and approached when working with children?

From an early age, children develop an evaluation about their world, from their internal and external interpretations as they are experienced. For some children, their external experiences may not correspond to their internal feelings. Subsequently, they may react to the external expectations more cautiously and struggle internally. These two primary sources can become so intermingled that it becomes difficult for children to separate what they have externally learnt and what they are feeling internally. These circumstances may lead to confusion and conflict. Children may then have difficulty in working out which is which, the permanent internal voice, learnt by external experiences, or their autonomous personal and true feelings (Smyth, 2013: 24). An example of this is when a child is told not to cry if they have fallen over because they will need to be 'big'. They are asked to suppress their emotions, and that everything will be ok. Therefore, when a child hurts themselves, they may feel they cannot go for comfort or support because it makes them seem like they cannot cope or are being too sensitive, evaluating other individuals' opinions about them and their behaviour. This in turn creates an attitude of anything that relates to pain which must be dealt with a sense of detachment and minimising attention and fuss. Internally the suppressed true feelings of wanting some attention and comfort may culminate in the way relationships are formed and certainly the way emotions are revealed and processed, within the individuals; feelings of self-worth and perceptions of others becoming a barrier to how children express what they really feel.

Rogers argues that as adults our sense of self is our own experience of what we find enjoyable painful and exciting. However, definitions of ourselves have often been imposed by our parents and other significant people, particularly in childhood, with some of these evaluations being conditional. For example, if you tell a child, you love them because they do not get angry, they may believe this. Love is conditional because it relates to not becoming angry. Unfortunately, what happens is that if anyone does get angry, it results in an incongruence between the self. This is based on others conditional regard and a person's concept of a sense of self based on their external experience. The concern for Rogers is that if a child believes the fear of losing love is when they get angry and for love to be consistent, feelings of anger should be avoided and blocked from awareness. As we know to develop as a healthy individual, all emotions are valid, including anger. For Roger, PCA deals in the here and now and helps clients restore their ability to become aware of themselves in a non-directive and unconditional way so they can explore unexpected expressions and whatever feelings they have. The therapist listens carefully and without interpretation (Smyth, 2013). They try to reflect on what they hear their clients saying with the aim to allow clients to become more aware of their feelings without being censored (Merry, 1999). Once clients realise that they can do this, a consistent sense of self remains and they no longer have the same need to shut off feelings, as they have done in the past, such as being angry. The aim is that the client will now be able to be more open to relationships and situations honestly (Tolan, 2003). They become more authentic rather than experiencing suppressed emotions as threatening or avoiding them. Roger considered psychological maturity is when a person can integrate significant experiences into a developing self. They then become capable of self-enhancement and growth. He sees this process of becoming as a continuous lifelong journey with clients being responsible for their own personal growth (Rogers, 1961). Rogers believes that clients often come to therapy in a state of incongruence, who they truly are and who they believe they must be to be accepted as a person. For him therapy accepts that a client may have a desperate need for external authority and part of the work of the therapist is to avoid falling into the trap by adopting the role as the authoritarian person, telling them what to do. Instead, the relationship is about walking alongside them on their journey of self-healing.

I consider this is something we can all do in our caring roles for children and each other. We provide the emotionally holding space for them but acknowledge that all emotions even uncomfortable ones should be recognised, felt and processed rather than avoided or suppressed, sometimes defined as being inappropriate behaviour. Rogers proposes that when we were young, we began to develop a self-concept, and this developed from the judgement and criticism of others who tell us that when we behave poorly or respond poorly. This self-concept is internalised so that we then reinforce it ourselves and act out how we think about ourselves. If we think we are worthless or un-acceptable, then we validate this through negative behaviour so that chances of then getting approval or esteem are further reduced.

An Example of Needing Some Support in Developing the Self

Sarah was always criticised for being too quiet and boring in comparison to her brothers. She was also criticised for not joining in with her brothers' activities, involving competitive sports. Subsequently she developed a concept of being quiet and a dislike for competitive sports. She would purposefully seek out ac-tivities that were quiet and less sociable as a way of validating her actions and sustaining her self-esteem. As she grew to adulthood, she met a partner who was more outgoing and enjoyed socialising. She began to feel like she was missing something and through talking to a counsellor following a bereavement, she began to realise she was struggling in her life socially and within work. She was considered a certain 'type' of person and by sustaining their approval, she tried to avoid any thoughts feelings or activities that would bring negative judgement on her. This meant that her relationships were conditional on behaving in a cer-tain way. By meeting a partner, she recognised an alternative and began to try new things, changing jobs, meeting new people and therefore behaving more confidently. In taking the risk of rejection by others regarding her more outgo-ing persona and verbalising what she wanted to achieve, she began to strive to-wards fulfilling her true potential. For many children growing up in loving and supportive environments, they generally receive the necessary nourishment of the actualising tendency. They develop the ability to trust their own feelings and thoughts and make decisions based on their feeling and desires. For those seeking an overwhelming need for positive regard, conflict and confusion lies at the root of much psychological disturbance. Decisions cannot be effectively made, and this can lead to a complete suppression of the self-actualising from the person experiences, leading to suppression of emotions.

Consider the Following Concepts of the Self

In considering a sense of self, Rogers evaluated three aspects of the self.

- Self-worth: Rogers believed that feelings of self-worth (what we think about ourselves) develop in early in our childhood and are formed through our interactions with parents and our home life.
- Self-image: How we see ourselves in relationship with our peer groups, workplace colleagues, our place within the family and other social groups to which we belong, and society in general.

- Ideal self: The concept of ourselves as we wish it to be in the future. This considers our goals, wishes and desires for ourselves and often changes throughout life (Maguire, 2019; Tolan, 2003).

According to Rogers, these three aspects of the self are fundamental in how an individual relates to their world. Rogers evaluated that personality was unique and ideas about collective stereotypes, as well as labelled personality types were inaccurate and unhelpful, especially to therapeutic work. He insisted on the validity of the individual experience in his approach (Maguire, 2019).

Focused Question

As professionals do we support the individual child in developing a sense of self-worth, a positive self-image of the self and support of their ideal self? Do we take an individual approach, or do we tend to generalise when we work with groups of children?

How does group care offer unique experiences within the micro-activities and routine during the day?

Relevance of a Rogerian PCA to Early Childhood and Play

Much has been written about pedagogies and development but broadly speaking in Britain contemporary early years practice aspires to be centred on the individual child as learner, in contrast to traditional subject-centred and teacher-directed approaches. The underlying principles of early years' pedagogy in early years' centres are based on a respect for the individual nature of each child, and the family and culture from which they come from. Children's physical development and their personal, emotional and social development along with their communication skills are seen as underpinning and supporting their intellectual development (Murray and Andrews, 2000). Early years practice is about sharing engaging, worthwhile experiences with children, linked to their interests and what they already know, thus scaffolding their fascination and wonder within their world. Children are motivated through active exploration of real and imaginary worlds; movement is essential for the growth of children's minds as well as their bodies. A well-planned nurturing environment supports children as active learners, provoking their interest and enquiry. It is dynamic, changing in response to children's prevailing concerns (Gully, 2014).

A Picture of Practice

A Familiar Part of an Early Year's Centre Is the Inclusion of Music and Rhyme

Finger Rhymes and songs have always been a popular feature of early years, forming a link back to traditional oral storytelling. The singing of finger rhymes is usually visible at certain times of the day. Familiar, repeated songs and rhymes are often passed down from practitioner to practitioner, with classic rhymes and songs often remembered fondly. For some practitioners, continuing the tradition of devoting time to share rhymes and songs remains an important part of a child's experience at nursery. The use of technology in music sessions has also marked a shift in how finger rhymes and songs have been delivered. While the use of, first tapes, then CDs and now more sophisticated audio sound systems are to be celebrated, there is, perhaps, a sense of a loss of simply singing and enjoying the human voice and the action of traditional nursery rhymes. In thinking about a PCA in this example, I have considered Froebel and how his principles aligned to a PCA.

Friedrich Froebel (1782–1852) had a passion for education and introduced some key theoretical thinking in early childhood. His theory of education was unique because he advocated mutual respect and holistic learning. He promoted an approach where children learned through experience and considered the individual rather than learning by rote, which was often a popular method at the time. Froebel considered 'Mother Songs' or as we now call them 'Family Songs' to be the starting point of developing the early physical skills of the body and senses. He also believed that, through these mother songs, a close emotional relationship could occur and that the mother/carer would feel that they were actively engaging, gaining a sense of rewarding responsibility in supporting the development of the infant in their care. Froebelian Principles therefore included the recognition of the uniqueness of each child's capacity and potential, a holistic approach to learning that recognises children as active, feeling and thinking human beings, seeing patterns and making connections, and learning that develops children's autonomy and self-confidence. In connecting to person centredness, finger rhymes offer an exciting opportunity to engage children as part of this dialogue. Froebel believed that repeating and re-telling finger rhymes was part of forming close bonds as well as contributing to the journey of more complex thinking and learning about literacy, such as story making. Today Trevarthen (2009 in Norman, 2015) talks about 'Motherese', the high-pitched tone of voice we use when talking to infants and how this musically influenced speech suggests a form of emotional communicative dance between both the mother/carer and the infant. In developing a deep rapport with positive regard towards the child, authentic and congruent relationships can be established and nurtured. Musical awareness is developed by communicating and expressing emotions, while, in turn, musical activity helps children to express themselves emotionally and develops communication. development occurs in unique ways when using finger rhymes that involve musical voice and finger manipulation (Norman, 2015) (Fig. 1.5).

PCA and Relationships in Early Years

As children grow, they develop significant attachments with adults both inside and outside the immediate family. A personal identity and the sense of who we are according to Bowlby (2005) are closely dependent on the few internal attachment relationships we have or have had in our lives. Upbringing

Figure 1.5 (a) and (b) Finger rhymes

influenced by those close to us can be secure or insecure, loving or neglectful (Bowlby, 1988). Therefore, close relationships are considered significant and influential to how a child makes sense of their world, as Carl Rogers high-lighted, self-actualising and being one with the self in adulthood comes from having relationships that emphasise the following:

- by being congruent with them
- providing unconditional positive regard
- having an empathic understanding (Rogers, 1980)

This is not just concerned with attending to emotional needs but also creat-ing opportunities for agency of voice, event with nonverbal infants, as illus-trated by Magda Gerber (2001) and Pikler approach (2010 in Gerber, 2001). Gerber believed that adults in western countries had become too interested in doing everything to or for a baby rather than allowing the baby their personal freedom to find their own way (Gerber, 2002). She shared the desire to en-courage practices that were supportive of children and created opportunities for families to listen to the child, allowing them to be active.

Picture of Practice

Listening to Children

Emily was a child who was having 'severe tantrums' as defined by her mother, and not responding well to school life. She was four years old. She felt she was not being listened to.

Figure 1.6 Communication and listening to feelings through drawing

Emily's physical world was disrupted when her father went away on nights, during the week, for work during the same time, she started school. Emily felt she was being sent away from home because her dad was away. It was important for Emily's mother to remember the daily plan organised and why she was feeling this way, her feelings of disruption and inner turmoil. By reflecting in this way, the behaviour was not considered a tantrum but an emotional state, a feeling of loss, loss of the home and loss of the father, loss of control. By working through this together, with the teacher Emily's mother gained an understanding why she was behaving in this way and helped her to reconceptualise Emily's emotions, offering different mediums for her to express herself, such as drawing, painting and being outdoors more. Although Emily's behaviour remained challenging, with unconditional support, Emily would be able regularly reconnect her attachment to her mother and override her senses of disruption that schools seemed to present (Fig. 1.6).

Carl Rogers described the therapist as a facilitator and for many theorists although facilitator may not be the termed used the practitioner or teacher's role often aligns to this conceptual understanding when working with young children.

A Person-Centred Toolkit for Practice

A Focus on How Pioneers Thinking Informs Present Practice

Explore these familiar pioneers in history and link how a CCA formed their theory and pedagogies, what is the role of the professional practitioner in

these approaches, and do they align to the areas of a PCA discussed in this chapter?

What further readings could you engage in?

Rachel McMillan *(1859–1917) and Margaret McMillan (1860–1931) recognised the value of first-hand experience and active learning through play. They emphasised the importance of health, and parents were closely involved in their open-air nursery which opened in Deptford in 1914.*

Susan Isaacs *(1885–1948) in 1924 founded the Malting House School, devising an environment and curriculum that was to stimulate the child's powers of curiosity and inquiry, and where children's intellectual development and emotional behaviour were to be observed and recorded in naturalistic surroundings. Observations were central to understanding children.*

Jean Piaget *(1896–1980) believed that learning comes though active involvement in the environment. Children progress through three stages of learning: 'assimilation', 'accommodation' and 'equilibration'* (NurseryWorld, 2012; Nutbrown and Page, 2013).

A Final Note

The benefits of this chapter were to gain an understanding about PCA and its application to therapy and counselling. By reading about the client–therapist relationship, there is an understanding about how the principles could be supported in education context. The approaches of being sensitive, listening in the here and now as well as investing in long-term relationships underpins a PCA. Understanding how individuals influence and are influenced by others are important areas to think about. Children have received many messages during the pandemic and what is expected of them. In developing ways to approach one-to-one care and listening to children, a PCA is a valuable approach with credibility, not just within therapeutic relationships, but also in early education.

The individual child is at the heart of the approach and while Axline (1974) highlighted working as a counsellor or play therapist is a specialised and unique job, a therapeutic approach, supporting emotional and social development of children would benefit all those caring for children.

The PCA is therefore framed by

- Congruence/honesty
- Empathy
- Understanding

Many practices and pedagogies in early years' centres align to a PCA and within humanistic psychology. It is concerned with the nurturing of individuals well-being and emotional health, and by understanding and applying a PCA, practitioners have the potential to 'tune in' and 'see' the child, particularly when working in-group contexts.

This chapter ends with the acknowledgement to how emotions can be supported as well as what is internalised by the child. By valuing a PCA, the emotions of the chid as well as the practitioner are valued, with a deeper understanding about how relationships are understood and therefore enhanced. The next chapter focuses on therapeutic play and how a PCA can be understood as a way of reflecting and developing early years' play practice.

References

Axline, V. M. (1974) *Play Therapy*. New York, NY: Ballantine Books.

Bekerian, D. S. and Levey, A. B. (2002) *Applied Psychology; Putting Theory into Practice*. Oxford: Oxford University Press.

Bowlby, J. (1988) *A Secure Base: Clinical Applications of Attachment Theory*. London: Routledge.

Bowlby, J. (2005) *The Making and Breaking of Affectionate Bonds*. London: Routledge.

Clare, T. (2018) The Symbiotic Relationship between Mindfulness and Person-Centred Therapy. Thresholds. *BACP Journal*. April 10–14, cited in https://chesterrep.openrepository.com/bitstream/handle/10034/621087/BC324%2520Thresholds%2520April_2018_10-14_02.pdf?sequence=4&isAllowed=y#:~:text=don%27t%20already.-,Both%20the%20theory%20of%20person%2Dcentred%20counselling%20and%20that%20of,their%20own%20way%20of%20being) (Accessed 28/08/2021).

Corey, G. (1996) *Theory Practice of Counselling and Psychotherapy* (2nd ed.) (pp. 89–129, 196–219). Pacific Grove, CA: Brooks/Cole Publishing Company.

Dryden, W. and Mytton, J. (1999) *Four Approaches to Counselling and Psychotherapy* (Chapter 3). London: Routledge.

Dryden, W. and Reeves, A. (2013) *Handbook of Individual Therapy*. London: Sage Publications [Thorne (2013)].

Gerber, M. (2001) *Respecting Infants: A New Look at Magda Gerber's RIE Approach. Zero to Three*. National Centre for Infants, McGraw-Hill. ISBN 978-0-9637902-3-1 [Pickler, (2010)].

Gully, T. (2014) *The Critical Years: Early Development from Conception to Five*. Northwich: Critical Publishing.

Hoffman, E. (1994) *The Right to Be Human: A Biography of Abraham Maslow*. Cochrane, AB: Four Worlds Press.

Horvath, A. O., & Symonds, B. D. (1991). Relation between working alliance and outcome in psychotherapy: A meta-analysis. Journal of Counseling Psychology, 38(2), 139–149. https://doi.org/10.1037/0022-0167.38.2.139

Horvath, J. (2021) *Louder than Words*. https://medium.com/the-creative-mind/carl-rogers-on-therapy-reconciling-internal-conflict-1c80bb811979 (Accessed 28/08/2021).

Kelly, K. (2017) *Basic Counselling Skills: A Student Guide*. London: Counsellor Tutor Ltd.

Lyon, H. C., Jr. and Rogers, C. R. (1981) *On Becoming a Teacher*. Columbus, OH: Merill.

Maguire, L. G. (2019) *Carl Rogers on Therapy & Reconciling Internal Conflict*. https://www.teachearlyyears.com/images/uploads/article/therapeutic-play.pdf (Accessed 14/09/2022).

Maslow, A. (1962) *Toward a Psychology of Being*. Martino Publishing.

Maslow, A. (2022) *A Theory of Human Motivation Paperback*: Wilder Publications (Accessed 31/08/2022) [Maslow (1973)].

McCormack, B. and McCance, T. (2016) *Person-Centred Practice in Nursing and Health Care: Theory and Practice* (2nd ed.). London: Wiley Blackwell [Smith (2013)].

Mearns, D., Thorne, B. and McLeod, J. (2013) *Person-Centred Counselling in Action (Counselling in Action Series)*. London: Sage.

Merry, T. (1999) *Learning and Being in Person Centred Counselling*. Ross-on-Wye: PCCS Books.

Murray, L. and Andrews, L. (2000) *The Social Infant*. Richmond, London: CP Publishing.

Norman, A. (2015) Rhyming with Froebel. *Early Years Educator*, 17(3). Professional normal in https://www.magonlinelibrary.com/doi/pdfplus/10.12968/eyed.2015.17.3.32?casa_token=TcQ-7Rd8pAUAAAAA:jSai0Y7_lO7q01T20Zm2O5t_r5w1N2hDEQglu06g8Z5p6kEjbYp00S2ChT1mW2M1RCJ6U3qdr-4 (Accessed 04/12/2020).

NurseryWorld. (2012) *Early Years Pioneers*. www.nurseryworld.co.uk/early-years-pioneers).

Nutbrown, C. and Page, J. (2013) *Working with Infants and Children*. London: Sage.

Phoenix, A. and Thomas, C. (2002) *Mapping Psychology*. Milton Keynes: OUP.

Rogers, C. R. (1951) *Client-Centered Therapy: Its Current Practice, Implications, and Theory*. Boston, MA: Houghton Mifflin.

Rogers, C. R. (1961) *On Becoming a Person: A Therapist's View of Psychotherapy*. Boston, MA: Houghton Mifflin.

Rogers, C. R. (1980) *A Way of Being*. Boston, MA: Houghton-Mifflin.

Rogers, C. R. (1983) *Freedom to Learn for the 80's*. Columbus, OH: Charles E. Merrill Publishing Company, A Bell & Howard Company.

Sanders, P. (2021) *First Steps in Counselling*: An Introductory Companion (5th ed.). London: PCCS Books.

Smith, M. (2004) Self-direction. *The Encyclopedia of Informal Education*. http://www.infed.org/biblio/b-selfdr.htm (Accessed 14/09/2021).

Smyth, D. (2013) *Person-Centred Therapy with Children and Young People*. London: Sage.

Steenbergen, E. E., van der Steen, R., Smith, S., Bright, C. and Kaaijk, M. M. (2013) Perspectives of Person-Centred Care. *Nursing Standard*, 27(48), 35–41. doi:10.7748/ns2013.07.27.48.35.e7799.

Tickell, C. (2011) *The Early Years: Foundations for Life, Health and Learning*. www.gov.uk/government/uploads/system/uploads/attachment_data/file/180919/DFE-00177-2011.pdf (Accessed 15/11/2021).

Tolan, J. (2003) *Skills in Person-Centred Counselling & Psychotherapy*. London: Sage.

2 Person-Centred Practice

Therapeutic play and supporting emotional well-being in early years practice

This chapter begins with an exploration about therapeutic play and the specialist role of the play therapist. Specifically, Axline's principles of play therapy will be considered, derived by the person-centred approach (PCA) of Carl Rogers. She is recognised as developing non-directive play therapy. Her well-known book 'Dibs: In Search of Self' was written in 1964 and described how she worked with Dibs, a young child, during a length of time. From the clinical work of Axline, reflections can be made about how a PCA could be included within early years education such as how the child should be encouraged to share their own account of their play with open questions. Emotional well-being is then discussed with reference to how the practitioner, while not a play specialist, could also engage in promoting good mental health and emotional well-being. The process of engagement, how body language is mirrored and the way practitioners are tuned into the child's play, without interfering or making judgemental statements will be discussed.

History of Play Therapy

During the twentieth century, several forms of play therapies have developed and evolved, including non-directive play. The origins of play therapy date back to the early 1900s with several early psychoanalysts, including Sigmund Freud (1928) who considered play as a modality for expression which can actively suspend reality. By suspending reality, he asserted that it allowed a child the freedom to make-believe play. Play being the medium of expression similarly to that of language in adulthood (Schaefer, 2011). Similarly, Anna Freud (1928) extended her father's work and emphasised that the implications of a child's play are more ambiguous than that of spoken language. For her play provides the opportunities in revealing the child's psychology, observed and analysed by the therapist (Schaefer, 2011). Klein's {1932} (1997) theory also considered that the content of play should be regarded as a vehicle for interpretation of a child's unconscious material (Schaefer, 2011). Non-directed, child-centred play therapy emphasises the importance of the therapist considering the child's view (Smyth, 2013). In considerations of the three core conditions, empathy, genuineness and unconditional positive

DOI: 10.4324/9781003272526-3

regard for therapeutic change, developed by Carl Rogers (1951), Axline developed eight principles of play therapy.

Axline's (1947a [1974]) eight principles of play therapy:

1 *Develop a friendly relationship*
2 *Accept the child without question*
3 *Establish the relationship as permissive so that the child can freely express their feelings*
4 *Recognize and reflect the child's feelings*
5 *Maintain respect for the child's problem-solving skills*
6 *Let the child lead and avoid directing the child*
7 *Let the session progress naturally, without an agenda*
8 *Make only necessary limits (Axline, 1974a [1947]: 73–74)*

Many studies have explored the effectiveness of play therapy and its benefits with children. In 1988, Landreth (1991) wrote, 'A therapeutic working relationship with children is best established through play, and the relationship is crucial to the activity we refer to as therapy. Play provides a means through which conflicts can be resolved and feelings can be communicated' (p. 11). Landreth conveyed a deep and enduring respect for children and their innate potential for growth and change at their own pace. Through a unique relationship that genuinely honours a child's capacity to self-actualise, Landreth refers to therapeutic objectives rather than setting specific goals within play therapy. According to Landreth (1991), 'the objectives of child centred play therapy are to help the child.

• Develop a more positive self-concept
• Assume greater self-responsibility
• Become more self-directing
• Become more self-accepting
• Become more self-reliant
• Engage in self-determined decision making
• Experience a feeling of control
• Become sensitive to the process of coping
• Develop an internal source of evaluation and
• Become more trusting of self' (p. 80)

According to Landreth (2002), 'children learn six main skills from the play therapy relationship:

1 To accept themselves
2 To respect themselves
3 To assume responsibility for themselves
4 To be creative and resourceful in confronting problems
5 Self-control and self-direction

6 To make choices and to be responsible for their choices' (Landreth, 2002: 283). These six skills are therefore considered beneficial for a child's over-all growth in maturity.

Theory of Play Therapy

Play is widely recognised as a way children can express their feelings and con-sidered an essential aspect of their development. Play is important because it 'transmits and communicates the child's unconscious experiences, desires, thoughts and emotions' (British Association of Play Therapy [BAPT, 2013, n.p].).

As children engage with their environment through play, their experiences enable them to express their thoughts and emotions non-verbally. Both direc-tive or non-directive approaches can be used in play therapy, as explained by Axline: 'Play therapy may be directive in form and the therapist may assume responsibility for guidance and interpretation. It could also be non-directive, and the therapist may leave responsibility and direction to the child' (Axline 1947, cited in Gill, 1991: 35). Often, and in the examples within this chapter, a non-directive approach allows the child to process their emotions at their own pace and creates the space for them autonomy to manage their environ-ment in the way that best suits them. Non-directive play therapy allows the child to regain a sense of control to a child when often their time is perceived beyond their control. Making choices and leading the play situations provides time for children to lead and make sense of their own needs during the ses-sion. As a theoretical model, play therapy aims to use the therapeutic powers of play to prevent and resolve psycho-social difficulties and assist the child in achieving optimal growth and development (Jensen et al., 2017).

The Play Therapist: A Day in the Life of a Specialist

A Play Therapist Working in the Community

Many play therapists have more than one job during a typical week, and this is an example of what a typical week may involve for a play therapist.

Pen Profile

The play therapist has two part-time jobs, both located in the education sector. They work as part of a Behaviour and Education Support Team and for a Behav-iour Support Team across several primary schools. Like many colleagues, they are considered a travelling play therapist with a transportable playroom. In schools, they would work with children who are likely to be excluded due to their be-haviour as well as children whose emotional needs have had a serious impact on their learning experience and social interactions. They also liaise with their parents/carers, teachers and other professionals involved in their care. As part of their role, they may also offer consultations to teaching staff and team members and act as a link to the local Child and Adolescent Mental Health Service.

Play Therapist Working in a Nursery

Pen profile

The play therapist may have worked in early years settings and had previous roles such as safeguarding or as a special needs co-ordinator. In seeking to explore more specialised training, this may have led to play therapy training. When working in an early year setting, the play therapist may select a time during the nursery day where they can focus on one to one with little disturbance and noise. When play therapists work with younger children, they may also be working with children that have mild-to-moderate needs rather than severe and for short time frames. Play therapy may be to support the child through a transition, such as a new family member or moving house. The play therapist will often use separate resources and objects as symbols to that of the setting, even if they appear similar. This is to ensure there is a distinction between the equipment played within play therapy. At the end of sessions, a small-scale report is written and shared with the parents and carers. Having talked to the parents and the staff, they feel they are part of the early years team.

A Play Therapist Working in a Primary School

Pen Profile

As part of their role, much of the play therapist's role and time within a school environment is based within individual play therapy sessions; they occasionally work with a whole class, using therapeutic methods or with a parent and child together. They may work in a person-centred way, which involves direct but more often non-direct approaches. Integrating the processes and the medium of play in a relationship-based therapeutic intervention connects development, learning within a therapeutic way (www.bapt.info/).

The Play Therapist Training within a PCA

Led by licensed and specialist play therapists, the aim of their specialised role is to provide a safe, supportive environment for children to play out concerns and difficulties, as well as helping children feel heard and understood. Play therapy aids the development of promoting healthy expression of the child's emotions and actions (Drewes and Schaefer, 2010). Being able to reflect on a child's emotions and actions is a specialist technique that plays therapists use to create an environment of open expression and understanding, as well as to enhance a positive therapeutic alliance between the therapist and child. It is therefore important that the therapist assists and facilitates the child's experiences. Play alone may not generally produce a change in the child; it is the interventions and applications of therapeutic play that arguably increase the likelihood of promoting emotional change within the child (Gill, 2019). The play therapist needs to be actively engaged in what the child is doing and communicating within a safe space and acknowledging that their feelings matter. Play therapists undertake rigorous academic and clinical training before qualifying. To be registered as a play therapist in the UK, they would be qualified through a university-approved postgraduate course, as well as clinically supervised, attending regular accredited professional development courses, and have an enhanced DBS check. Play therapists would also be registered with the professional standards authority, an independent organisation regulating and monitoring health and social care providers.

Therapeutic Benefits of Play

As already discussed, play therapists are a specialist service and profession. Bearing this in mind a practitioner working with children would still be supporting and understanding their emotional well-being and mental health through play. Alison Hestletine (2021), an Early Years' Service Officer, considers how crucial the role of play is to healthy development, underpinned by the Early Years Foundation Stage Curriculum in England (EYFS, 2021). During the pandemic, play has also been therapeutically valuable for children to express themselves and process external events. As Hestletine evaluates, play builds a sense of trust and connection with others through shared, sustained ideas and experiences. It creates a safe place where thoughts and feelings both of joy and frustration can be expressed without words. Play offers opportunities to be calm and focused, making sense of the world. Play also enhances self-confidence and resilience as children learn to deal with challenge as well as enabling children to feel a sense of control. Children are therefore learning to self-reflect and self-regulate their thoughts and feelings, supporting their emotional development but also teaching them to create a sense of calm for themselves (Hestletine, 2021).

Children can also re-visit real-life experiences and try to make sense of them, bridging the gap between a child's perceptions and reality. Having opportunities to do this in a safe space has a lifelong impact as children apply new abilities such as self-expression and emotional regulation to other areas of their lives. In observing children's play, recognition is in the knowledge that play belongs to children and recognising and respecting their choices, and individuality is crucial (Hestletine, 2021, Smyth, 2013).

Working closely with aligned specialists, including play therapists, can also guide practitioners to a deeper understanding and appreciation when undertaking observations and reflecting on play practices and outcomes. Reading about children engaged in therapeutic play can also widen knowledge about the value of play and opportunities offered in educational and care environments.

Picture of Practice: A Case Study of the Role of the Therapist

The child I was engaged with was four years old and was challenged in expressing how they felt.

Figure 2.1 (a) and (b) Sand and objects (symbols) can be helpful for story-making and supporting communication

They were playing with sand during a training play therapy session (Fig. 2.1a,b).

At the beginning of the session, I introduced my name and the time frame we would be working within. I also said I would give them a few minutes warning at the end if they wished. I attempted to do this in a calm way to allow the child to feel I was behaving in a friendly and warm way at the start, supporting Axline's basic rules. I wanted to create a quiet calm meeting, ensuring it flowed even though I, as a play therapist, was feeling a little anxious.

I also started the session by discussing the boundaries of the session. I explained that if anything was discussed, it was confidential unless it was something that caused me concern and then I would have to tell the appropriate person. I also explained the health and safety issues such as the space is theirs to explore and do as they wish within a set of boundaries. If they started to do something that was dangerous to the environment or to themselves, they would then be given a warning. If they continued, then another warning would be given and if after that the session would be stopped. This was also in line with Axline's basic rules of giving a few limitations – anchor to reality – but making sure the child was aware of their responsibilities, again attempting to do this in a warm and friendly way. As a play therapist, this was quite challenging because there was a need to be approachable but also establishing the guidelines at the start, so the child was aware of the parameters of the session. As this was explained, the child approached the sand tray. They explored the tray with their hands and moved through the sand slowly, sifting it between her fingers. They asked if this was ok to do and I replied yes, allowing them to establish a feeling of permission to do what they wanted. They then asked if they could select some toys and again, I asked if they wanted to get some toys. They went to the toys and asked what a particular object was that they picked up. This was a shell. My initial reaction was to state what it physically was but as a therapist I needed to not only mirror back but reflect on their actions and words so that child gains an insight into what they want it to be rather than what it is labelled as. They took their time exploring the toy taking one back and then returning.

I knew at this point the time frame was limited but again had to ensure I was considering Axline's basic rules of not hurrying the process but allowing them to take the lead without the concern of time.

They then returned to the sand and moved the sand with the objects stating:
'I can't do this'
'I don't know what to do'

As a play therapist I had to allow the child to take responsibility for making the choices of toys and allow them to lead. This was something that may have been what they wanted me to do, directing them in their activity. I had to consider that it was for them to lead with careful questioning I asked
'You don't know what to do?'

This was one way of responding. Another way I felt was to say as little as possible so the child could then decide what it was, they actually didn't know what to do because although they were verbalising this, they were actually exploring the materials and 'doing' quite a lot with the sand. I used eye contact and mirrored their body language to allow them to feel comfortable. They had also selected a toy dog and stated this was like the one they had at home. I went to answer that it was a big dog and what was their dog at home like but then stopped halfway. I realised this may not be a dog but something else and to say as little as possible was best to allow them to lead the conversation and be more reflective than analytical towards their play. When they were selecting the symbols (objects) they seemed unsure, submissive trying to get me to choose the toy. I had to try to get them to select by stating I was not sure either and asking them for help. This was quite challenging. I had to both be myself and be aware of slipping in and out of the therapeutic situation when I was being spoken to. This was particularly evident when the child asked about her mum was returning. I had to say the time. During the sand exercise I felt I asked a few leading questions and as a therapist I need to ensure I follow Axline's basic rules by allowing them to lead within the time frame given. I was calm throughout and said they had a minute left of the time. This was ignored but when I told her the time was finished, she asked if they could return and I felt that being warm and friendly, and although was receiving quite hostile responses was beneficial to developing a rapport.

As an illustration, this example demonstrates how I felt and processed in the here and now, as a therapist creating a safe space. I noted in my narrative that I was worrying about saying too much or interpreting when they asked about the toy. I also noted that when they did not know what to do it was very tempting to jump in and answer with suggestions, while sometimes it is better to simply stay quiet and allow the child time to process their own thoughts. I was also trying to listen to their words, rather than interpreting her feelings, or in some cases misinterpreting.

Focused Question

How many times do we navigate the play as a practitioner working in education?

Do we allow space for 'quietness' and 'slow' thinking or do we jump in to fill the gaps for the child?

In my own practice, I personally found this exercise initially challenging and reflected that although I think I am child centred in my approach and a good listener I was actually quite directive and things were ok as long as I navigated the play … not that helpful for the child! This led me to reflecting on the whole child and how holistic play is conceptualised by the child and if this aligns or differs from a child's own understanding about their play (Fig. 2.2).

A PCA within Early Education

Approaching **holistic play** to support emotional well-being and good mental health, within a PCA, is the thread within this chapter. By understanding and exploring play therapy, the key principles of a PCA can be drawn on by the practitioners working with young children in formal day care. Boyer (2016) summaries that a PCA can be implemented into early childhood education, because many of the underlying beliefs and principles about both PCA and early childhood education align. The important social and emotional attributes required to become successful begin in early child development with practitioners supporting their behavioural and emotional regulation (Smyth, 2013). Similarly, PCA is concerned with the trust and empowerment of human

Figure 2.2 Person-centred early education practice

beings to be able and willing to connect with others, both socially and emotionally (Boyer, 2016). Rogers' (1951) core principles of congruence, unconditional positive regard, empathy and genuineness should be available in a nurtured, understood and appreciated environment with adults to promote positive personality changes in children (Boyer, 2016).

While the intention is not to suggest, a practitioner can be a therapist or counsellor, as these require specialised training the principles of being able to be genuinely present, accessible, engaged, interested and focused on the immediate experience of the child or client are achieved in both roles. Like counsellors, who often engage with empathy to understand what it must be like to be their client, early childhood educators also regularly reflect from the child's perspective in a bid to understanding their social and emotional support needs. Axline (1947a [1974]) considered one of the important factors in supporting the mental health of children within schools is through relationship building. Therefore, if early childhood educators are given the knowledge, tools and techniques to establish positive relationships with their children, they can be just as effective in providing positive development. Axline (1947b) also recognises the permissiveness and the facilitative role of the teacher and how they acknowledge the child's feelings. This gives clarification to what children think and feel, enabling and encouraging them to retain their self-respect and the possibilities of growth and change. Friendliness and warmth on the part of the practitioner also develop good rapport between her and the child and this was seemed to individualise the child even when instruction is given to a large group at any one time.

A Case Study of Kindergarten Teachers Employing Play Therapy Principles

While this was a more directed approach, then PCA does offer a window to how non-directed play therapy principles can be acknowledged, understood and researched.

Example 1: The Sunshine Circles is a teacher-led group process using social-relationship principles from Theraplay. This study was conducted across six preschool sites in the midwestern United States. Interviews with teachers confirmed that the intervention subjectively increased classroom cohesion, teacher-student relationships, and improved behaviour (Tucker et al., 2017).

School teachers implemented the program, offering and promoting safe, caring, engaging and participatory learning environments for children with social-emotional difficulties. The aim was to build self-esteem and support learning.

Example 2: Messy play

Gascoyne (2018) is a play therapist by profession and has developed and published a book on Messy Play. This provides a rich tapestry to how messy play can be transformative and provide opportunities for development and

Figure 2.3 (a) and (b) Messy play: clay

*agency. As a guide for practitioners, it celebrates the way play can be theoreti-
cally informed and understood within messy play. Through observations and
guidance, it provides a source of engagement about the deeply significance
of sensory engagement through play (Fig. 2.3a,b and 2.4).*

By reading and adopting this approach to messy, play practitioners can develop their play practice and reflect on the therapeutic benefits for children's
social and emotional development and well-being.

Example 3 Toy Free Kindergarten in Munich

*The setting removed all the toys and equipment in the setting and decided
to focus on open-ended resources with the children to engage in. Practitioners evaluated that they acquired new ways of connecting with the children in
their care and it became more child-led inquiry based. There was also more
attentive trust. They followed Axline's eight Guiding principles and noted how
some aligned with mainstream practice, while other principles questioned
their practice (Gascoyne, 2019: 182) (Fig. 2.5a–c).*

Figure 2.4 (a) and (b) Messy play: paint

Figure 2.5 (a)–(c) The story of the stone, using loose parts as treasure to play

Focused Question

This may be considered a dramatic approach, and would settings consider this in the UK and if they have already what have been the outcomes to this form of play without toys?

Decisions about Therapeutic Play in an Educational Context

While it is recognised therapeutic play can be supported by practitioners and teachers, this is not considered a replacement for specialist services. Practitioners and teachers are present and central to observing when a child they know needs extra support for educational, social and emotional reasons. Many children will at some point experience a difficult time in some way, and this can often be resolved within the school staff team using existing resources and experienced staff. However, if more time and support and specialist knowledge is needed than the teacher is able to offer in the classroom, then referring them to a play therapist can be of value (https://playtherapy.org.uk/for-teachers).

The Practitioner's Role in Early Years Settings Supporting Emotional Well-Being and Good Mental Health though Play within a PCA

Principles of Play Therapy within a Key Person Approach

By drawing on Axline's eight principles guides as highlighted earlier in this chapter, and now extended, consider how they could be part of the early year's community in the way the practitioners interact with the children in their care:

1 *Develop a warm and friendly relationship with the child.*
2 *Accepts the child as she or he is.*
3 *Establishes a feeling of permission in the relationship so that the child feels free to express his or her feelings completely.*

4 *Is alert to recognise the feelings the child is expressing and reflects these feelings back in such a manner that the child gains insight into his/her behaviour.*
5 *Maintains a deep respect for the child's ability to solve his/her problems and gives the child the opportunity to do so. The responsibility to make choices and to institute change is the child's.*
6 *Does not attempt to direct the child's actions or conversations in any manner. The child leads the way, the therapist follows.*
7 *Does not hurry the therapy along. It is a gradual process and must be recognised as such by the therapist.*
8 *Only establishes those limitations necessary to anchor the therapy to the world of reality and to make the child aware of his/her responsibility in the relationship (Gascoyne, 2019: 182–193).*

These principles not only describe the play therapists' approach, but they also draw parallels to the way practitioners work with young children in their settings. The practitioner in their role, as a key person, working in centres such as formal day care, uses a range of play and relational pedagogical approaches to support young children's emotions. Babies and children become attached to significant adults within reliable, respectful, warm and loving relationships which are essential to thrive (Norman, 2019). Babies and children experience well-being and contentment when their physical and emotional needs are met, and their feelings are accepted. The key person approach in their close relationships with families helps to meet these conditions. Informed by Bowlby's attachment theory of human development of attachment theory it focuses on the bond between a caregiver and a care seeker to establish security and coping skills (Norman, 2019). By understanding attachment with play, this theory is important because it emphasises the value of the adult's presence and the effectiveness of the practitioner as a key person. Bowlby describes attachment is a system of regulation, whereby caregivers and care seekers maintain an accessible relationship for support and comfort, especially during times of stress (Bowlby, 1988). Attachment theory therefore provides a powerful system of connection between people (Riley, 2011). The practitioner's role in early years' settings is to help the child to feel known, understood, cared about and safe. The practitioner's role involves a triangle of trust with the child and family. An effective practitioner approach needs to include strong leadership and committed practice. The key person helps the child to feel known, understood, cared about and safe. They support the baby or child to feel confident that they are emotionally held, thought about and loved. This experience of being cared for by reliable adults who meet their physical needs and remain attentive and playful, affectionate and thoughtful allows children to form secure attachments. By providing a 'secure base', children begin to feel confident to explore the world and form other relationships (Elfer et al., 2011; Norman, 2019).

Focused Question

Read the following ten principles of a practitioner's role in their capacity as a key person. How do they compare with Axline's eight principles highlighted earlier?
Can you identify differences and similarities within the professional roles?
Principles of a key person in early years

1 *Has passion for their work and sees the value and rewards in being a key person*
2 *Has empathic and understands the different ways of creating a family*
3 *Appreciates and respects the cultures, identities and diverse backgrounds of the children and families with whom they work*
4 *Able to draw on their own informal knowledge of childcare practice from within their own experience and reflect on how best to use or build on it*
5 *Able to reflect on and understand the influence of their own attachment experiences on their work with children and families, with the confidence to know when to ask for support and further training*
6 *Willing to research and reflect on the concept of 'professional love', so that they can see its relevance to their work as a key person*
7 *Not judgemental and has the skills to communicate with other agencies and settings involved with the child and their family*
8 *Has wider knowledge and understanding of, for example: child development attachment theory, including social and biological factors that might affect a child's capacity to form attachments co-regulation and self-regulation neuroscience (brain development and how it links with all the prime areas as well as self-regulation and executive function) pedagogy of effective, relation-based practice*
9 *Identify and support children in a range of circumstances, including those who are vulnerable, looked after, with visible and invisible special educational needs and disabilities*
10 *Recognises that it is a personal as well as a professional relationship which brings with it much joy, as well as challenge (Birth to Five Matters, 2021, n.p.).*

In early years, education children are encouraged to engage in a variety of play-based activities related to cognitive understanding. However, emotional literacy is just as important to nurture and create time for children to develop. For children, play is not only an activity but a method of communication, through which they can express themselves, their thoughts and their opinions about the world. Play is children's language, through which they tell their own stories which they may have difficulty putting into words. By the telling of stories, they can reshape their experiences. It is a child's natural way of recovering from their personal daily emotional challenges and processing the feelings and outcomes of events in their lives. Like any other language, play requires the user to spend time to develop it. Children, therefore, need space inside and outside, company to communicate with, props such as toys and or real objects to learn to manipulate and symbolise (Horvath, 2021).

A PCA Approach to Play

In play, a child can explore their thoughts and feelings in creative and dynamic ways, without having to use words to articulate themselves. In play therapy sessions, children explore their own creativity and express themselves using media such as: drawing and painting, water and clay, sand tray and miniatures, guided imagery, relaxation techniques, as well as drama and puppetry, poetry, movement and music. Talking about problems can be too challenging for children, perhaps restricted to time and space boundaries in the setting. Furthermore, a child may not have the words to describe how they are feeling, or why they are behaving as they do. They may not be able to recognise what they find difficult or able to explain themselves. Play provides the expertise and time to do and can support their ability to develop healthy and resilient relationships, and to work though traumatic experiences which may be preoccupying them. Pre-occupying difficult feeling can make learning or managing feelings challenging. Addressing difficult emotions through play could be through sharing a story or metaphor. Strategies such as the use of metaphor can provide a degree of removal from experience for the child. It can allow the child to feel safer to express themselves and explore their experiences through play (Smyth, 2013).

The aim of play through a PCA is to support child's everyday play, communicate with them and allow space for them to understand themselves and others. Furthermore, a PCA also recognises and supports children's needs to cope and develop resilience in their feelings of anxiety and frustration, improving their capacity to trust and to relate to others. A range of play activities can be used to promote the expression of feelings and emotions. Expressive arts, the use of clay tends to promote the expression of aggression, sorrow and concern, as it allows children to be creative, and it's through this creativity that emotions are likely to emerge or be expressed. Drawing, for example, allows children to get in touch with their inner self and can be used to illustrate the development of their strengths. Children can be asked, for instance, to create a representation of what is troubling them, what makes them feel contented or what they would like to say. Finger painting can promote emotions of joy, celebration and happiness. Imaginative pretend play may help children to learn about social skills and observe situations in a safe environment. Puppets and soft toys can also be helpful when learning and practising behaviours. By getting involved in puppet play with the child, adults can mimic situations that motivate children to respond in a variety of ways, so the children can indirectly explore the appropriateness of their own social behaviour. An imaginary journey taken with the children, a personal story, allows them to get in touch with their memories to relate critically to their perception of the

Figure 2.6 Soft toys

events, through dramatic role play. Miniature animals and sand play provide visual pictures by encouraging children to talk about whatever may be troubling them (Horvath, 2021; Smyth, 2013) (Fig. 2.6).

More Play Experiences within a Person-Centred Approach

Therapeutic Play and Music

Singing is conveyed by many parents to their infants in societies around the world. Lullabies have, across many cultures, had the dual aims of passing down cultural traditions as well as helping parents to express their own feelings. However, evolutionary theories have also suggested that singing to infants has potentially evolved from motherese, the way parents talk with their infants. This is generally exaggerated speech melodies and frequent repetition as a mechanism of reassuring infants and promoting parents-infant bonding (Trevarthen, 2000).

From a therapeutic perspective, music has been a central aspect to supporting the well-being of infants' relationships with both parents and practitioners in developing emotional connectivity. In using a PCA, a practitioner can respond and allow the infant to take the lead, using music and song as a means of communication in creating the present moment, in tuned and listening.

Picture of Practice

Consider the following activities introduced and implemented in an early year setting that could support and encourage a PCA.

Loose Parts

In the setting, loose parts were both gathered randomly or organised with a purpose by a practitioner. Loose parts were also led by the children themselves gathering items. These included a combination of wooden materials, such as rings, cotton reels and other items such as bags of shells, twigs and buttons. The intention of these was for the children to use them individually or together. The open-ended resources encouraged a sense of wonder and there was dialogue between the practitioner and child in how things worked, why they felt a certain way, how it made them feel and what connections could be sought. In celebrating the children's own ideas, Bruce (2012) talks about how first-hand experiences can encourage symbolic play, nourishing the child's inner life and express understanding (Fig. 2.7a,b).

Wooden Blocks

In the setting, both open-ended materials such as blocks were available indoors and outdoors. The larger blocks were frequently played with and through

Figure 2.7 (a) and (b) A collection of loose parts in a sand tray to create a story

Figure 2.8 (a) and (b) Wooden block

reflective observations; the practitioners noted the children encouraged mean-ingful talk and engagement between themselves. The negotiation of where to put the bricks and helping each other developed a sense of working together and resolving problems and issues. As a small community, they talked together rather than their frustration taking over. With the availability of the practitioner nearby to support how risks could be taken in the building, the children also developed negotiation skills. With encouragement and support, the children considered how each other felt emotionally. They began supporting each other rather than focusing on what was going wrong in the build. The blocks simplicity and aes-thetic appeal encouraged children to use their imaginations to create whatever they wished. There was also no hurry in achieving a result so often seen in cur-riculum activities. These open-ended resources actively enabled the children to master their play, though a process and this was evident in their play (Fig. 2.8a,b).

Mirrors

In the setting, mirrors were placed in different spaces and in part, used as a means of identification and self-reflection (Fig. 2.9a,b). They provide a use-ful medium in engaging children in abstract thinking and symbolic thinking about themselves.

1   How do they feel when they view their own face expressing in different ways?
2   How does it feel to see our own face?
3   Are we comfortable in self-exploration?

Sensory Spaces

Silk drapes or curtains were also placed in different spaces to evoke different feelings and being enveloped within the area. The use of fabrics, texture and colour contributed to how the children responded to the space and physically experienced it. The children learnt how to hold up the fabrics, the weight

Figures 2.9 (a) and (b) Mirrors and play

of the fabric and how they could hide within them. The children were particularly interested in den making and creating spaces to hide. Small group friendships were formed in the intimate spaces rather than parachute play, which was often to entice everyone to join in (Fig. 2.10a,b).

These activities and resources were included to illustrate how they may be implemented and interacted with and by the children. In the Smedley and Hopkins (2020) project, they noted that practitioners evaluated with harmony came joy and connectedness between their environment and those engaged within it. They agreed there was no prescribed 'way' of using resources rather, the central purpose was for the children to explore and adapt to them as they wish. Smedley and Hopkins (2020) evaluated that the practitioner's found resources were engaged with differently by the children when they themselves were thinking about how to support children's emotions rather than managing their behaviour. They discovered that when they gave more autonomy to the children in what they wanted to play with the children engaged in the resources, in a much more fluid 'play time'. They also recognised there was much more agreement and contentment between the children when they played.

Focused Question

Are the activities discussed familiar in early year centres?

Do they resemble a PCA and include principles of empathy, understanding and congruence.

What other practice sand activities could be considered when reflecting on a PCA in early years settings?

Figure 2.10 (a) and (b) Drapes to divide and encase spaces

A Person-Centred Toolkit for Practice

Therapeutic Play and Engagement: Hypothesis Maker within a Dancing Dialogue

A relational pedagogy requiring sensitive, responsive caregiving that relies on attunement and intersubjectivity. It recognises that while pedagogy is played out in the here and now, it also stretches out to the in-between spaces that connect to the past as well as to the future. A key implication of this pedagogy is therefore the necessity that practitioners remain reflective and critically engaged with their pedagogy and its potential for long-lasting impact (Liston and Zeichner, 1990; Palaiologou, 2021). Throughout the day and already considered in the previous chapter music is a communicative tool for infants to become aware of the time of day, transitional times and support both the infant and practitioner in creating or maintaining a routine.

A PCA and Classical Music at Rest and Sleep Time

During rest and sleep time at a centre with babies cared for, selected classical music pieces was played at a low level to enable the infants to respond, creating a calm ambience without overstimulation. Some infants found it challenging to relax and sleep during the day, becoming quite stressful. The inclusion of specific music created a calm and relaxing atmosphere within the room.

Lullabies, for example Brahms' Lullaby, was played to lull infants to sleep or slow things down a little. Classical music was therefore considered beneficial for infants through co-regulation to begin self-regulating their behaviour and bodies to music (Varvara, 2012). In practice, the music also enabled an infant to take the lead in how they feel and act accordingly at times of the day, such as quiet times. Listening to music was part of several strategies including rocking an infant in a practitioner's arms or swaying to the rhythm as a way of tuning into them, bonding and interacting through individualised approach.

The Role of the Adults: PCA from Practice to Policy in an Early Year's Centre

A PCA and developing ways to support children's emotions, rather than managing behaviour, enables the practitioners to feel supported and confident in their own abilities allowing for expressions of feelings to occur naturally and be explored rather than corrected or measured. Changing policies such as behaviour management to emotional supportive policy re-conceptualises the language used to label children. Changing the language used and reflecting on experiences are essential if educators are to develop thinking about the inner child, rather than behaviour surrounding children.

'Children need encouragement as growing plants need warmth and light, and they must have parents' love and understanding' (Bruce, 2012: 20). Listing to the child and being a facilitator throughout the process acknowledges their choices and allows freedom with guidance. Sharing the reasons about why different types of behaviour occur can relieve a lot of home tension and stress. Bruce (2012) affirms that in the long term, the development of the inner child will result in empowered individuals of tomorrow.

The Practitioners

Relationships with others are key to the learning process. This includes sensitive and positive relationships between children and adults. Free movement, free choice and self-activity are important but within a framework of guidance in which the role of the adults is guiding and supportive. The environment should be safe and intellectually challenging, promoting creativity, friendships, enquiry and adventure. Practitioners should be attuned to the individuality of the children, their learning and development within the environment. This can be achieved by

• Ongoing and regular observations being central to understanding the children cared for
• Knowing children's spontaneous play and learning are reciprocal: understanding more about children and the practitioners own understanding about play in development and the value placed on learning and development

- Recognising the inner good of the child and the reason for behaviours
- Gaining confidence in recognising the good and nurturing possibilities in play rather than rewarding intermittent behaviours

A Final Note

This chapter ends with not just how emotions can be supported but also what is internalised by the child and in valuing a PCA. Emotions of the child and the childcare practitioner can be better understood and therefore enhanced by the knowledge of specialist services as well as how therapeutic play could be part of the everyday life of the children cared for. The next chapter, therefore, focuses on the emotional child and the PCA as a way of reflecting and developing practice.

References

Axline, V. M. (1947a/1974) *Play Therapy*. New York, NY: Ballantine Books.

Axline, V. M. (1947b) *Dibs in Search of Self*. New York, NY: Ballantine Books.

Birth to Five Matters. (2021) https://birthto5matters.org.uk/attachment-and-the-role-of-the-key-person/Attachment and the role of the key person.

Bowlby, J. (1988) *A Secure Base: Clinical Applications of Attachment Theory*. London: Routledge.

Boyer, W. (2016). Person-Centered Therapy: A Philosophy to Support Early Childhood Education. *Early Childhood Education Journal*, 44, 343–348. https://doi.org/10.1007/s10643-015-0720-7

Bruce, T. (2012) *Early Childhood Practice: Froebel Today*. London: Sage.

Drewes, A. A. and Schaefer, C. E. (Eds.). (2010) *School-Based Play Therapy* (2nd ed.). Hoboken, NJ: John Wiley & Sons.

Elfer, P., Goldschmied, E. and Selleck, D. (2011) *Key Persons in the Early Years: Building Relationships for Quality Provision in Early Years Settings and Primary Schools* (2nd ed.). London: Routledge. https://doi.org/10.4324/9780203804711

Freud, A. (1928) *Introduction to the Technique of Child Analysis*. New York, NY: Nervous and Mental Disease Publishing.

Gascoyne, S. (2018) Messy Play in the Early Years: Supporting Learning through Material Engagements 1st Edition, London. Routledge

Gill, K. (2019) *How Play Therapy Treats and Benefits Children and Some*. Adultshttps://www.healthline.com/health/play-therapy (Accessed 14 Dec 2022).

Hestletine, A. (2021) *National Week of Play: Harnessing the Therapeutic Value of Play*. https://www.eyalliance.org.uk/national-week-play-harnessing%C2%A0-therapeutic-value-play

Horvath. (2021) Louder than Words. https://www.teachearlyyears.com/a-unique-child/view/therapeutic-play

Jensen, S. A., Biesen, J. N. and Graham, E. R. (2017) A Meta-Analytic Review of Play Therapy with Emphasis on Outcome Measures. *Professional Psychology: Research and Practice*, 48(5), 390–400. https://doi.org/10.1037/pro0000148

Klein, M. (1997) The psychoanalysis of children. London. Vintage

Landreth, G. (1991) *Play Therapy the Art of the Relationship.* https://www.brightstar-therapy.co.uk/history-of-play-therapy (Accessed 10 Oct 2022).

Landreth, G. (1991/2002). *The Art of the Relationship* (2nd ed.). New York, NY: Brunner Routledge.

Liston, D. P. and Zeichner, K. M. (1990) Reflective Teaching and Action Research in Preservice Teacher Education. *Journal of Education for Teaching,* 16(3), 235–254.

Norman, A. (2019) *Conception to Two. Development Policy and Practice.* London: Routledge.

Palaiologou, I. (2021) *The Early Years Foundation Stage: Theory and Practice.* London: Sage.

Riley, P. (2011) *Attachment Theory and the Teacher-Student Relationship.* New York, NY: NY Publishing.

Rogers, C. R. (1951) *Client-Centered Therapy: Its Current Practice, Implications, and Theory.* Boston, MA: Houghton Mifflin.

Schaefer, C. E. (2011) *Foundations of Play Therapy* (2nd ed.). Hoboken, NJ: John Wiley and Sons.

Smedley, S. and Hoskins, K. (2020) Finding a Place for Froebel's Theories: Early Years Practitioners' Understanding and Enactment of Learning Through Play. *Early Childhood Development and Care,* 190(8), 1202–1214. https://doi.org/10.1080/03004430.2018.1525706

Smyth, D. (2013) *Person-Centred Therapy with Children and Young People.* London: Sage.

Treats and Benefits children and some. www.healthine.com. Accessed. 22 Nov 2022

Trevarthen, C. (2000) Musicality and the Intrinsic Motive Pulse: Evidence from Human Psychobiology and Infant Communication. *Musicale Scientia,* 3, 155–215. https://doi.org/10.1177/10298649000030S109.

Tucker, C., Schieffer, K., Wills, T. J., Hull, C. and Murphy, Q. (2017) Enhancing Social Emotional Skills in At-Risk Preschool Students through Theraplay Based Groups: The Sunshine Circle Model. *International Journal of Play Therapy.* https://dx.doi.org/10.1037/pla0000054

Varvara, P. (2012) Supporting Parent-Child Interactions: Music Therapy as an Intervention for Promoting Mutually Responsive Orientation. *Journal of Music Therapy,* 49(3), 303–334. https://doi.org/10.1093/jmt/49.3.303

3   Person-Centred Care

An emotional pedagogy with young children

This chapter examines a person-centred approach (PCA) and the way it supports the emotions of the young child and their emotional literacy. It also includes the value of a PCA and how it can support an emotional pedagogy and highlights some aligned pedagogical approaches that already place the child at the heart of education and care in early years centres. A PCA recognises the importance of valuing their voice and connects to the United Nations Convention of the Rights of Child. Emotions will be explored in relation to young children's mental health and well-being, with a call for further attention to develop and implement an emotional pedagogy in formal day-care settings.

Valuing the Person

In everyday life for most people, the word person is used merely as the singular version of people. In a PCA, the word person is of greatest interest because it aims to capture those attributes that represent what makes us individuals as a human. It is concerned with the way we construct our way of life how we think about moral values how we express our political self, spirituality or religious beliefs. It also considers how we engage emotionally and in relationships. The concept of a person from this perspective is therefore shaped by how people relate to each other in developing a sense of self (McCormack and McCance, 2010: 325).

The word person has been debated for as long as philosophical thought has existed, and for some philosophers, it is not enough to claim human beings are persons based on a collection of their physical and psychological attributes. Today a person's uniqueness as humans can be distinguished by their ability to engage in reflection regarding their actions. In person-centred therapy, the person contributes to co-creating their social world, with the growing awareness of how they have often manifested and contextualised their personhood (Rogers, 1980). For those in therapy, the focus is often on letting go and losing a sense of themselves and why they acted and thought in a certain way. They may also display irrational behaviour during this therapeutic journey in trying to make sense of their personal experiences as well as their own responses to them (McCormack and McCance,

DOI: 10.4324/9781003272526-4

2010: 325). In considering relationships beyond therapy and thinking of the child, their behaviour and thoughts can also appear to the carer as sometimes irrational or lacking engagement. By reacting and responding to their environment, the process can also be a sense of trying to understand their outer world and the messages conveyed around them. Rather than focusing and defining the child by their behaviour, they should be respected for their intrinsic worth and value in developing a sense of self in a secure and safe environment.

The Beginning of Emotional Relationships

In creating environments of feeling wanted, nurtured, loved, protected and valued by emotionally available and sensitively responsive carers, the child gains a sense of emotional well-being. They can reach their full capacity to form and maintain relationships and a richness of language to socially communicate. Parents can be supported in understanding what is expected physically and emotionally about themselves and their developing relationships. Effective, timely, consistent, and non-judgemental prenatal support culminates in parents gaining a sense of being better prepared for their transition into parenthood. For the baby in utero, their brain is rapidly developing and responding to diet, exposure to stress maternal health and lifestyle. As the brain develops, the foetus can respond to familiar sounds and tune into their parent's voice (Kisilevsky et al. 2009). Brain development is accelerated by this sensory input, forming grooves and ridges on the brains surface, leading to the thickening of the cerebral cortex and myelination. Myelination is the fatty sheath coating of neurons, which enables quick information processing. The development of myelination contributes to higher order brain regions that control feelings, thought and memory. The key factor here is that in facilitating myelination, the experiential input of regular positive experiences, stimulation of play and sensory development all contributing to brain development (Conkbayir, 2017). By describing the growth of the brain, it draws attention to the close link between brain development and the influence of varying external contexts exposed to, known as the emotional brain. This is helpful to know when considering how a PCA could support the developing child through sensitive interactions. If the mother or other close consistent carer is well attuned to the infant and responsive to their needs, this can support their development.

Evidence from brain development research suggests

- Elevated stress hormones can be hazardous to the brain, dampening electrical activity
- Very young infants experience large cortisol (stress hormone) surges during aspects of daily care (undressing, bathing)
- Sensitive care buffers cortisol surge: sensitivity impacts on a child's development (Eliot, 1999 in Blakemore and Frith, 2005)

Parents and practitioners who have responsibility for infants and young children should have some understanding of the 'brain story' in developing their own pedagogical choices about care and approaches within the environmental context. Responsive caring and in my view acting on increased knowledge about the growing brain and emotions as well as person-centredness can promote caregiving buffers against infant stress, wiring up the brain positively for learning and emotional literacy (Campos et al., 2004).

A Growing Sense of Self and the Influence of Others

A loving environment includes support and positive reinforcement to guarantee the nourishment of emotional growth. This relates to a person's developing awareness to be able to trust their own thoughts and feelings and make decisions according to their valuing processes, enabling them to move through life with a sense of satisfaction and fulfilment. Those experiencing unsupportive relationships and suffering from the imposition of many disciplinary conditions of worth develop an overwhelming need for positive regard. They may desire a desperate need for approval in determining their own valuing processes. External negative responses may therefore create inner bewilderment that undermines their confidence and be challenged by making effective decisions (Gerhardt, 2004).

Observing the Emotions of the Child as They Make Sense of Their Strange External World

A child surrounded by those who are sharply critical and judgmental will struggle with their own value of self-worth and their self-concept. Even if they can disregard these feelings, they may still have difficulty in making personal decisions being able to articulate and make sense of their own feelings. A reliance on guidance by external authorities or desperate attempts to please anyone may result in unpredictable, inconsistent and incongruent behaviour (Axline, 1974 [1947]; Stonehouse, 1989; Taggart, 2015). A child's self-concept develops through the process of acting and then reflecting on themselves and others' feedback. This reflection is based on actual and possible actions in comparison to one's own expectations and the expectations of others and to the characteristics and accomplishments of others (Brigham, 1986). That is, self-concept is not innate but constructed and developed by the individual through interaction with the environment and reflecting on that interaction. Through exploring these areas of the self in a trusted relationship, the individual recognises their own patterns of behaviour and the emotional attachment to them (Fig. 3.1). Perhaps they can reflect on what has initially triggered such behaviour and those significant around them.

Figure 3.1 (a) and (b) Inner feelings: self-regulating with the outer experiences

How Can We Promote a Good Sense of Self with the Children We Care for?

Self-esteem is the affective or emotional aspect of self and generally refers to how we feel about or how we value ourselves (one's self-worth). Self-concept can also refer to the general idea we have of ourselves (Huitt, 2009).

Directed Question

How could a PCA positively enhance self-esteem with children we care for? How can we promote an environment that nurtures self-worth?

A Person-Centred Educational Space

Childhood, specifically in the UK and beyond, is considered an important and unique period regarding their emotional regulation (Boyer, 2009 in Boyer, 2016). Rogers (1942) maintained that individuals have the capacity to become who they want to be with the support of others who genuinely care about them and try to understand them, being unconditionally accepted within supportive environments where children are assumed to be trustworthy resourceful capable of developing a self-understanding and direction. A PCA, therefore, encourages the natural expression of warmth loyalty and trustworthiness within relationships, listening and accepting individuality of a person. Authentic relationships are built, and the core conditions can be fostered to provide positive change for children. The practitioners are attuned to the emotional and social needs of young children enabling them to increase their self-understanding self-appreciation self-confidence as they begin to understand appreciate and trust others. There are various factors that predict the development of self-regulation in young children. The first is a strong attachment to primary carers, or as PCA refers to as 'unconditional positive regard' from the adults in their lives. Therefore, practitioners are emotionally available to the child and not directed by the child's behaviour. By being emotionally available and professionally loving the child in their care, they are caring opportunities for the child to face challenges, take risks in a safe, holding environment. In nurturing this space, children then develop agency of voice and can take the lead in their own behaviour. By allowing children to take and manage risks, becoming independent and resilient, the child develops self-regulation rather than relying on the practitioners to lead their behaviour and thinking; 'co-regulation' with practitioners supporting and nurturing them. This can range from talking calmly to the child to allowing freedom of choice within the play offered. Some children may need more support and will struggle with the idea of waiting and being patient, or in empathising with their peers.

Sue Cowley (2021) considered the role of the practitioner role in supporting self-regulation and asks for them to consider and reflect on the language used when interacting with the children and put trust in the children as well as inviting the children to trust them.

Within this framework, the focus is on caring communities and how this has and can be enhanced through play pedagogies with a focus on emotions (Fig. 3.2).

Creating Person-Centred Caring Communities in Formal Early Years Education and Care Settings

The focus of this chapter is caring communities and opportunities for personal growth become a natural part of the early classroom. Philosophically early childhood educators provide children with opportunities to consider themselves beyond their behaviour. Children with varying personalities need to feel welcome and feel comfortable. This encourages the child to be open to new experiences, learning new things and finding new ways to invest in themselves. They may also demonstrate trust in themselves by believing that they can do something and use and orchestrate their own direction and process. Practitioners provide children with interactive experiences that demand more action orientation such as blowing bubbles, colouring or taking a walk and sharing thoughts and feelings about their life events. These types of experiences are a necessary part of early childhood learning because they provide opportunities for children to gain sensory experiences of the world and joy. In all the activities available and engaged in over time, the child can discern what is enjoyable and comforting for them as well as safe and socially appropriate and they learn

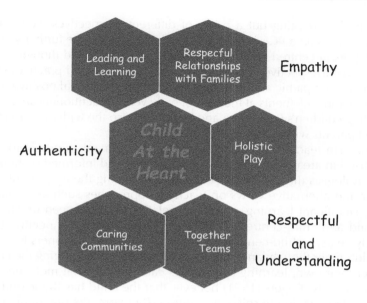

Figure 3.2 Person-centred early education practice (PEEP)

to actualise these positive experiences for themselves. Rogers (1992 in Rogers and Freiberg, 1994) believes that creating rapport creates a safe and welcoming environment and facilitates the individual's courageous acceptance of self and the respectful acceptance of others' end person-centred therapy, this request that they are being modelled the golden rule to treat others as you would like them to treat you.

Connections to PCA and Other Pedagogical Approaches

Despite a much greater tolerance for freedom of thought and engagement in the early years and other educational sectors, there are also increasing neoliberals that demands twenty-first century practitioners to justify their educated practices. As a reaction towards often accountable pressures, increased attention has gone to alternative ways of thinking about relationships. It also invites resistance to the kinds of top-down approaches perhaps considered more suited to an older child. A PCA is a valuable way of supporting learning and aligns to other approaches with a humanistic perspective (White, 2015: 46). By considering other aligned pedagogical approaches, a PCA is strengthened to how caring and educating children could be approached.

Similarly, pluralism, as discussed by Cooper and McCloud (2011), has many approaches, philosophical and pedagogical conceptions in early years education. There is no one privileged perspective from which we think we should all be adopting but a prism of different perspectives. Furthermore, this does not mean a PCA is diluted but rather a PCA can be further validated through person-centred practices. Therefore, what is agreed though in using a PCA is that irrespective of curriculum and pedagogies, all practices should be authentic, empathic and include a sense of unconditional positive regard. With these three elements at the core of early years, practitioners are not only supporting children's well-being and health but also the wider community of staff and parents within the community it serves.

Humanism teaching theory is based on the humanism psychology and is practised in areas within educational contexts and informed by humanistic psychologists (Jingna, 2012). Humanism teaching theory presents some familiar and alternative views on teaching approaches such as self-actualisation, significant learning, emotional relationships between practitioners and child and child-centred teaching (Maslow, 1943). Connecting this to the early years, a child-centred approach promotes practitioners to care for the child's inner thought and treat them equally. By encouraging the child to discover their own, learning approaches can explore what motivated them to learn actively. Rogers (1951) believes that the child has the learning potential and motivation to self-actualisation. Therefore, the practitioner's task is not to teach the child how to learn, but to offer and facilitate learning processes, and the child learns by themselves. The practitioner should not live as 'practitioner' but a more of facilitator and, by doing so, can reduce the often-psychological intense atmosphere created by external influences and pressure about what they are capable of learning and achieving.

Focused Question

The first year of entering a school culture is often around the child being school ready. Consider and reflect how the environment can be child ready through a PCA.

What key attributes do the practitioner and teachers need to consider themselves in their approach?

In Rogers' (1951) view, the 'child-centred' in educational contexts is the same as 'client-centered' in hospitals. The practitioner should get the child's trust in same way the doctor treats and is trusted by the client. No matter how the child thinks, the practitioner should treat their views with empathy and establish emotional communication with them. To apply the theory to early years education, some basic steps could be followed:

1 Let the child decide the content and the motivation of learning by themselves. In motivating the child to learn, the practitioner considers the content of what they are delivering and pay attention to the child' individual needs, taking the lead from them. The practitioner can guide the child to arrange their learning activity and, at the same time, the practitioner can offer some useful and necessary conditions.

2 The child masters their own learning approach.
   The practitioner's important task is to support the child how to understand what works for them and their approach to obtaining and experiencing the world.
3 Let the child evaluate themselves.
   A child' self-evaluation is the vital consideration to establish learning independence. Using self-evaluation can help the child know how they have learned and whether they have achieved their aims, and then how to make progress.

Picture of Practice

Rachel was four when she arrived at school, having recently had her birthday in August. She was quiet and did not volunteer to speak or contribute in other ways. She appeared exhausted most of the day and began to increasingly cry as she was left at the school by her parent. The following year she had settled a little better and had some friends but continued to be quiet and withdrawn although participated in activities. Her understanding of concepts was considered immature at this stage, and she was encouraged to do 'maths' and read every night to develop her 'letters' She had an assessment that year on her reading, nonsense words and phonic words. She did not achieve the assessment standard and the school talked to her parents at home about her work. The following year she was set to do the assessment again and again she failed. By this time, she was six years and in her second year of school. With the continual focus on targets and assessments, she would 'switch off' and cry every day when she went to school. The educational psychologist was notified and asked to support. He asked her what she liked about school and what she found difficult. She liked her friends, liked being at home, cooking and going to the park. She didn't like learning and couldn't see the point of it. She did not like maths as she didn't understand it and reading was hard. She wanted to play and be at home as she felt stupid and people knew ... the school thought she may have dyslexia but the educational psychologist concluded she needed encouragement and time, with activities to motivate and ignite enjoyment. He noted some areas observed showed inconsistency in a specific learning difficulty.

Focused Question

Reading this case study: reflect on the age of beginning school, the curriculum offered, the accountability of national assessments, the child's position and the specialists involved. Consider how Rachel's first three years were experienced.

The humanism teaching theory considers the research on cognition, emotion, interests, motivation and potential of the child during the process of learning. It encourages practitioners to think for the child and promote them to feel the interests and enthusiasm in learning. Humanistic psychologists believes that the child's self-actualisation and the creative ability are their vital factor for their behaviour. The material, social and cultural environment will promote of stop the realisation of the potential. In conclusion, humanism considers the understanding of the child' inner voice of thought and how they express their differences and individuality in interests, needs, experience and personality (Buhller and Allen, 1990).

By extending the humanism teaching theory to early years education, a consideration of European approaches is considered. The Reggio Emilia approach, based in North Italy and developed by Malaguzzi, advocated a need to embrace all individual children and the languages that they bring to learn and play with. The United Nations Convention on the Rights of the Child stated that children have the right to be listened to and have their voice heard (Robinson, 2014 in Hart, 2004). This was written into the compulsory document of the Department of Education, making sure all practitioners were hearing children's voices and were able to express themselves in any way they feel comfortable (Robinson, 2014 in Hart, 2004). From this, it is signifying that making sure children were listened to was crucial to children and the education system.

In Reggio Emilia, children are advocated to have freedom and express themselves within the community they live and are educated. 'Young children are particularly attracted to narrative, creating stories, becoming part of imaginary situations and copying real life through role-play. They need the freedom of space to do this' (Valentine, 1999: 19). 'The environment should ... encourage autonomous thought and encourage and maintain action' (Valentine, 1999: 19). By teaching children to improvise and encourage them to use their initiative during play, children will learn this skill and use it in the future. This approach focuses heavily on documenting the children's learning as well as allowing the children to really take on their interests. The parents and educators, as a community, are there to support the learning process of the child over the time that they are there at a Reggio or a Reggio-inspired centre. The learning approach is through child-led projects that are open-ended. Children are given certain concepts that they need to solve through research, questioning and experimentation. There is a strong focus on the arts, which is a vehicle to allow the child to express and contemplate their thoughts and emotions through multiple mediums (Gandini et al., 2005).

Contemplative pedagogy is also used broadly to refer to a third way of knowing that complements the rational and the sensory. The contemplative mind is opened and activated through a wide range of approaches. This is from, pondering to poetry, to meditation, designed to quiet and shift the habitual chatter of the mind to cultivate a capacity for deepened awareness, concentration and insight. Although various practices may evoke different kinds of awareness, such as creative breakthrough or compassion, they share a distinct nonlinear consciousness that invites an inner opening of awareness, akin to a PCA. This opening within, in turn, enables a corresponding opening toward the world experienced. Through a fresh lens, our worldview, sense of self and relationships may be powerfully transformed. Various contemplative approaches also focus on different goals, for example, calming versus insight contemplation, each dividing into critical and creative types (Thurman, 1994). Translated into early classroom aims, various approaches may evoke creative imagination, critical reflection or concentration and may use the gateway of silence, poetry, the body or other means, as we will explore. Contemplation also can nourish the practitioner's own presence (Miller, 1994 in Miller and Cable, 1992; Solloway, 2000 in Hart, 2000) and subsequently influences the quality of the classroom experience. A practitioner who explores their own contemplative mind is better able to help his or her child to do the same. The practitioner-child dynamic is enhanced through this mutual exploration, and ultimately the practitioner's own growth transforms the entire space in which education happens.

Contemplation Case Study: Playing with Mud

Children should have opportunities to engage in a variety of sensor experiences and this may include engaging in materials less familiar to the practitioners. By engaging with mud, the practitioners and children can explore the activity together, considering how a PCA could be included as a way of opening up a conversation about mud play. Key questions could be asked about their thoughts of the medium as well as observing how the children are engaging in the sensory activity. Opportunities for self-reflection and attitudes towards natural mediums are also a good way to consider what the practitioner is feeling and how they are portraying their emotional responses to the medium before the children in their care (Fig. 3.3).

Focused Questions to Ask Yourself as a Practitioner

- Do you consider mud as fun, dirty, messy, creative, dangerous, exciting or mysterious?
- What are your own experiences of playing with natural mediums such as mud?
- How could you facilitate and play with children that is authentic and supports their needs as they engage with something perhaps less familiar to the adults?

Initiating regular dialogues with the team about specific activities can promote a more PCA to the way they are facilitated and responded to with children by evaluating these activities and practitioners' responses to them could provide evidence to how a PCA could be developed in meaningful and practical ways. This seems relevant, bearing in mind practitioners follow a 'relational pedagogy' which is sensitive to the social and emotional needs of young children (Taggart, 2016). It draws on social and philosophical thoughts on the topic of compassion as a way of seeking to show how this concept also applies to early years work. Most recently (Taggart, 2019a), empirical

Figure 3.3 (a)–(c) Playing together with mud and clay

research in the emergent field of 'compassion science' provides a rationale for a programme, which could aim to foster compassion in trainee practitioners. Interventions to cultivate compassion have typically drawn upon mindfulness practice and this can be included in an early year's context (Taggart, 2015) alongside reflective practice and a deliberate focus on adult attachment styles (Taggart, 2019b, 2001, 2004).

Another pedagogical approach is the revival of slow pedagogy. A slow pedagogy, coined in Honoré, the author of the popular book 'In Praise of Slow' (2004), described the pressure he felt on parenting to be one of the catalysts for investigating the value of slow as he felt himself tempted by the idea of the '1 min bedtime story' for his child. Hurried parents and practitioners often result in hurried children. The psychologist Elkind (2001) first set out his concerns about 'the hurried child' in the 1980s. Several decades later, the pandemic has raised new issues about the relationship between time, everyday life and learning in early years. Attention has been on the need for 'catchup' and 'lost learning'. This has highlighted the fast-paced learning children experience. It also highlights the language of competition, of education as running a race. Children need to 'catch up' with their lost learning to meet the benchmarks set. Catchup is a visible and powerful indicator of the push toward accelerated childhoods. This idea of accelerated childhood contrasts with an implicit valuing of unhurriedness across early childhood traditions and the centrality of play. Therefore, increased focus has revived the concept of the unhurried child (Carlsen and Clark, 2022). This includes the conversations and reflecting on the dialogues between practitioner and young child through a PCA.

Bakhtin's legacy (1895–1975) has also left a rich platform for us to think about in relation to pedagogy, including slowing down today. He approached learning as the social experience between with encounters being less concerned with cognition in an intellectual conceptual sense. Rather, he considered relationship encounters as shaping consciousness. This focuses on the socially imbued nature of human beings in dialogue engagements with ideas (White, 2015: 35).

In a dialogical classroom, practitioner does not simply deliver or receive ideas. Teaching and learning is never fixed because it relies on individual interpretations and draws from many different implements. Dialogical pedagogy emphasise is the idea that dialogue is learning not merely a means to learning seen in this way. Dialogical pedagogy focuses on learning engagement with other questions and provocations rather than answers. The following principles underpin this approach:

- And infant space possible meanings
- A place where the curriculum is dialogue
- Contingent responsiveness to other
- Characteristic by a lively discussion about ideas of importers to learn this
- Interested invalid knowledge for a range of sources
- Resisted of endpoints interested in starting points of wondered
- Not afraid to set challenges or respond to those posts by others
- Concerned with ideas not the correct answer
- Welcoming of uncertainty
- Respectful of the space and style of communication learners bring to the classroom
- Underpinned by relationships that take time to try to under understand others
- Influenced by what can be seen and what is unseen but nevertheless important
- Respectful of diverse ideas and ideologies
- Encouraging of debate descensus perhaps even silence
- Interested in insiders' and outsiders' perspectives on topics
- At times, lots of fun at times potentially painful, sometimes both (p. 37)

In a Bakhtinian approach, there is more emphasis on teaching with love (p. 78) rather than the authoritative words of the authoritative adult. Kenneth

Greg (1999 in White, 2015) suggested practitioners are constantly immersed in multiple emotional flows within their pedagogical experiences. However, he reminds us that a child also arrives with multiple emotions. The complex emotional response relations require practitioners to be open to the multiple, constantly changing nature of learning, as well as valuing the many voices that are bought to play in any pedagogical moment. The practitioner should therefore be aware of their own emotions and emotional responses, spending time getting to know their child. Felt (2011 in White, 2015) explains simple strategies such as eye-to-eye contact as an appropriate means of conveying affection approval and establishing intersubjectivity for young children. Similarly, other facial expressions, such as the smile, are also identified as a significant source of reciprocal communication, the expression of positivity, although such interpretations may be culturally determined. These non-verbal language forms, coupled with verbal communications, play an important role in establishing the atmosphere that supports meaningful dialogue. The benefits of love in pedagogy are the benefits of paying attention with the fullest expression of understanding children, a challenge when caring for large groups of children. Relational pedagogies emphasise mutual relationships between young children their families and practitioners. Such approach relies heavily on practitioners understanding about the children's interests and prior experiences. By listening and watching them closely, interpreting their multiple languages and talking with their families' practitioners' personal views about what children learning relational pedagogy can be formed.

Within Early Years Pedagogies: A Person-Centred Approach and Practice through Daily Activities

In connecting many practices and pedagogies in the twenty-first century, a curiosity approach bridges many approaches and aims for children to return to their freedom, by igniting their natural curiosity and imagination. When adopting curiosity, children can think for themselves, make their own choices and direct their own learning. I have included some thinking around this approach as it aligns and underpins a PCA of being empathic, authentic and unconditional positive regard.

An approach underpinned by curiosity has been developed in England and coined The Curiosity Approach, as a credible pedagogical approach within early years education. It incorporates many of the approaches already mentioned, such as slowing down, making learning fun and allowing for freedom of voice and play. The curiosity approach is based on child-led learning with children encouraged to make their own choices, and solve problem for themselves, leading to enhanced confidence, critical thinking and problem-solving skills. The approach, therefore, includes practice from other philosophies of early education including Reggio Emilia, Montessori, Pikler and Steiner, with the aim to create children who are 'active agents instead of passive learners'. The environment plays a key part in this approach with classrooms decorated in neutral tones. This aims to evoke a peaceful, tranquil environment which does not distract away from a child's learning but instead places full focus on the various loose items which children can play with. The resources are placed at eye level and accessible. Rather than offering toys, classrooms offer loose parts to encourage children to use their imagination to work out what the item is. Therefore without guidance, it has the potential to increase their confidence and encourages them to think independently. The child may then be able to follow their own schematic learning styles as items can be lined up, counted, connecting play with learning (Hellyn and Bennett, 2022).

Developing Respectful Relationships

Loose parts are also used and encouraged so children develop more respect for different objects. By using natural materials, children learn concepts around handling the items with care and respect. Furthermore, an approach underpinned by curiosity also includes a range of authentic resources. The aim being for children to play with objects without feeling restricted. This promotes the idea that each child should be treated equally and is able to freely express their interests (Hellyn and Bennett, 2022).

As researcher and practitioner, I have been very fortunate for the opportunities to reflect and observe the way pedagogy has been approached with infants through an educare approach. Pedagogy is not only about the how and why of what early years educators do in their professional roles but also extends to the way educators engage with the expectations presented to them in their work setting. Infants learn best in atmospheres that provide a stimulating and prepared environment where children learn from their own perspectives (Lilley, 1967). In the setting time, planning areas for children to engage with their emotions and be cared for by a listening and observant practitioner is essential for development and well-being to occur. Aligned to some of Rogers' principles, Gerber (2003) considered respect as the basis of an educaring approach, demonstrating respect every time we interact with them. Respecting a child means treating even the youngest infant as a unique individual.

- An authentic child: An authentic child is one who feels secure, autonomous, competent and connected.
- Trust in the infant's competence: We have basic trust in the infant to be an initiator, to be an explorer eager to learn what he is ready for.
- Sensitive observation: To observe carefully to understand the infant's communications and his needs.

The more we observe, the more we understand and appreciate the enormous amount and speed of communication and how learning is communicated. In the many forms of communication young children may use (Gopnik et al., 1999), Malaguzzi referred to these forms as the 'hundred languages' of children (Edwards, 1999). An understanding of the many languages young children use enables the practitioner to listen to and communicate with children to gain an appreciation and better understanding of their emotions when interacting. Listening and recognising children's emotions therefore become more than a simple interactional engagement (Rinaldi and Samson, 2008). It requires reflections on the part of the practitioner about their own emotional state and the communicative approaches they use. Interpreting language and language as part of complex chain of utterances emphasises the unique meanings an infant may bring to the understanding. Through parental sharing, an understanding to language beyond the immediate context is also made and understood (White, 2015). 'Self-actualisation' is the education aim which is pursued by all the humanistic educators including Rogers. Rogers points out that what is the reason for people to learn, the only reason is to satisfy the self-actualisation needs. Self-actualisation is people's instinct need, and it is the most important inner motility, even the power to promote the society. The aim of education is to promote 'selfhood' to be realised. Therefore, self-actualisation becomes the basic education aim and Rogers emphasises that the aim of education is to foster open-minded, dynamic and adjustable people who know how to learn and continue to learn (Maslow, 1970).

Picture of Practice

Reflections of a Play Project Implemented that Aligned to a PCA in Practice, Supporting Children's Emotional Growth and Development

The understanding of children's emotions and how their associated behaviour could be supported and 'managed' has always been part of early years discourses, influenced both by contemporary thinking as well as histories and traditions (Norman, 2022). Friedrich Froebel (1782–1852) theory of education was unusual for his time in that he promoted mutual respect in children and allowed children to be themselves with self-expression and freedom (Lilley, 1967). Similarly, a PCA he advocated children learn through autonomy and the adult should begin with what the child is learning rather than directed and taught. All early years settings are required to document and engage in a behaviour policy, a document that sets an expected standard of behaviour associated with the values and customs of the setting. With demands of meeting standards, these policies tend to be unified, with opportunities to download pre-written policies with space in the text to personalise and edit so that it is recognisable as 'belonging' to the setting. Whist modifying an existing policy has its benefits, the creativity and reflective thinking around the content of creating a unique individual policy based around emotions rather than behaviour can build on the strengths of the child (Bruce, 2012). Through freedom of play, accepting there is some guidance, the child will create their own sense of self and develop an emotionally self-satisfying outcome without having to seek rewards externally. Planning, organising and preparing emotional spaces allow the child to freedom to explore within. Whilst creating emotional spaces to enhance emotions is a novel concept, existing spaces have existed, including Elinor Goldschmid's *Islands of intimacy*, creating opportunities for practitioner and child to engage in one-to-one conversations and Jarman's research of communication-friendly spaces, offered in early years centres. Personally, and collaborative emotional spaces can create opportunities for intimate and secure areas to explore feelings of self and others. By doing this, autonomy is enhanced through experiential learning valuing the child's voice and developing emotional literacy. The implementation of varied forms of emotional spaces was explored in a day nursery catering for children from birth to four years. The initial stages were recorded and with the help of the children are continually developing evoking new perspectives to how emotional spaces could be engaged with.

Person-Centred Toolkit for Practice: Introducing Creative and Collaborative Emotional Spaces within the Setting

In the setting, a wall display was created to encourage practitioners and parents to read Froebel's principles and contemporary values of a PCA's empathy, unconditional positive regard and authenticity. This was valuable in developing a sense of understanding about values and philosophy not just with the children but the practitioner's role too.

Initially, the setting up of the emotional space's consideration of colour space and light was explored. The blue created calmness and the feeling of being enveloped within the space. The use of fabrics, texture and colour contributed to how the children responded to the space.

Creating creative and collaborative emotions outdoors. The spaces were partitioned by moving material pending the weather to evoke reflective thinking about the elements and emotions.

This space was a prepared environment: the area was found to be more active in its aim: resources were presented, and the children physically moved around more – in this space, there was less enclosure and enveloping than in other spaces (Figs. 3.4a–c, 3.5a–c, 3.6a–c).

Figure 3.4 (a)–(c) Exploring and using fabrics in working together, being creative and being co-operative

Figure 3.5 (a) and (b) Learning together

Exploring Co-Regulated Areas: Policy to Practice

Collaborative co-regulated are areas within the classroom environment that celebrate and enhance emotional communication, forming friendships and listening to one another.

Emotional Spaces Can Include

1 Cushions
2 Drapes/Silk material to enclose part of the area or a tent of neutral colour to zone the area

Cosiness or comfort is often used to describe a vibe or feeling that you'd get from snuggling indoors on a cold day. Hygge in the early years is a Danish approach to life that focuses on living in the moment and enjoying every minute. It's not about having to buy new things but simply taking the time to enjoy the special everyday moments we have. In creating this space, comfort

Figure 3.6 (a)–(c) Leading others outside in the play dance with fabric in make-believe

is achieved through the soft furnishings and self-selected time to enter the space (Hellyn and Bennett, 2022).

Equipment within the co-regulated area: a sack of resources used and presented during each play session, as described in Chapter 2.

1 Puppets
2 Story books or fact books with emotions as a theme
3 Persona dolls
4 Open-ended materials such as blocks
5 Mirrors
6 Photographs/Pictures of faces with different expressions
7 Small pot of pens/paper
8 Personalised children's books (Fig. 3.7)

There is no prescribed 'way' of using the equipment rather the central purpose is for the children to explore and adapt to the co-regulated area as they wish. Play as central to learning in the premise that it is this bio-logical need of children to play in understanding how things work. Play is considered purposeful and experiential rather than an idle pastime. The co-regulated area within the classroom is a prepared environment with the materials listed above mindfully selected, rather than random with little thought in the process (Bruce, 2012).

Figure 3.7 Books and areas all about me

As Froebel evaluated, play environments include carefully considered and prepared equipment, presenting children with the tools and materials that are optimal for their level of emotions.

In creating spaces, in the nursery, we also thought about the entry and leaving spaces too!

Simple posters to evoke discussions about feelings can provide powerful imagery to allow children the opportunity to reflect on how they think. This walk area was to and from the indoor and outdoor providing imagery along the way beyond the typical friezes of numbers and letters frequently used.

The emotional environment areas allowed space for children to

- *Help each other rather than compete*
- *Participate in the rules and boundaries*
- *Opportunities for children to self-evaluate*
- *Create a value-driven environment: what ought to happen*

By creating emotional spaces, the children began to create their own spaces in their play; emotions became part of the repertoire rather than received by the practitioners. This was evident through the children's responses to each other and the way they were interacting and co-operating with each other. Their behaviour was less conflicting, and resolutions were becoming more apparent during play. Individuals were taking responsibility for their actions in creating the whole (Fig. 3.8a,b).

A Final Note

This chapter is helpful in gaining an understanding about PCA and emotional pedagogy. Rogers encouraged respect towards the child, encouraging them to think independently, and through this, they will become more confident.

Figure 3.8 (a) and (b) Creating spaces outside

As Rogers says, 'a man is a running program, not a cluster of solid material, he is a group of great potential changing all the time, not a group of solid character' (Jingna, 2012: 32–36).

On this basis, emphasis on the integration of knowledge and ability is central. This chapter ends with not just how emotions can be supported but also what is internalised by the child and in valuing PCA emotions of the child and the childcare practitioner can be better understood and therefore enhanced. The next chapter, therefore, focuses on the emotional child and the PCA as a way of reflecting and developing practice.

Further Readings

Axline, V. M. (1974) *Play Therapy*. New York, NY: Ballantine Books.
Blakemore, S. and Frith, U. (2005) *The Learning Brain*. Oxford: Blackwell Publishing.
Boyer, W. (2016) Person-Centered Therapy: A Philosophy to Support Early Childhood Education. *Early Childhood Education Journal*, 44, 343–348. https://doi.org/10.1007/s10643-015-0720-7
Brigham, J. (1986) *Social Psychology*. Boston: Little, Brown & Co.
Bruce, T. (2012) *Early Childhood Practice: Froebel Today*. London: Sage publications.
Bruce, T. and Meggitt, C. (1999) *Child Care & Education* (2nd ed.). London: Hodder & Stoughton.
Buhller, C. and Allen, M. (1990) *Introduction to Humanistic Psychology* (Chen Baokai, trans). Beijing: Hua Xia Publishing House.
Campos, J., Frankel, C. and Camras, L. (2004) On the Nature of Emotion Regulation. *Child Development*, 75(2), 377–394.
Carter, M. (2007) *Making Your Environment 'The Third practitioner* (pp. 22–26). London: Exchange.
Carlsen, K. and Clark, A. (Eds.) (2022) Potentialities of Pedagogical Documentation as an Intertwined Research Process with Children and Practitioners in Slow Pedagogies. *European Early Childhood Education Research Journal*, 30(2), 200–212. https://doi.org/10.1080/1350293X.2022.2046838
Cooper, M. and McCloud, J. (2011) *Pluralistic Counselling Psychotherapy*. London: Sage.
Conkbayir, M. (2017) *Early Childhood and Neuroscience*. London: Bloomsbury Publishing.
Cowley, S. (2021) *Learning Behaviours: A Practical Guide to Self-Regulation in the Early Years*. London: John Catt.
Dorman, H. and Dorman, C. (2002) *The Social Toddler*. London: Children's Project.
Edwards, A. (1999) Research and Practice: Is There a Dialogue? In H. Penn (Ed.), *Early Childhood Services: Theory, Policy and Practice* (pp. 184–199). Buckingham: Open University Press (2014).
Elfer, P., Goldschmied, E. and Sellek, D. (2011) *The Key Person Approach in Nurseries* (2nd ed).: London: Routledge.
Elkind, D. (2001) *The Hurried Child: Growing Up too Fast too Soon* (3rd ed.). Cambridge, MA: Perseus Publishing Cambridge.
Gandini, L., Hill, L., Cadwell, L. and Schwall, C. (2005) *In the Spirit of the Studio: Learning from the Atelier of Reggio Emilia*. New York, NY: Teachers College Press.

Gerber, M. (2003) *Dear Parent: Caring for Infants with Respect Resources for Infant Edu-Carers*. Resources for Infant Educarers.

Gerhardt, S. (2004) *Why Love Matters: How Affection Shapes a Baby's Brain*. Hove: Brunner-Routledge.

Goldschmied, E. and Jackson, S. (1994) *People under Three: Young Children in Day Care*. London: Routledge.

Gopnik, A., Melzoff, A. and Kuhl, P. (1999) *How Babies Think: The Science of Childhood*. London: Weidenfeld/Nicholson.

Hart, T. (2004) Opening the Contemplative Mind in the Classroom. *Journal of Transformative Education*, 2(1), 28–46. https://doi.org/10.1177/1541344603259311

Hellyn, L. and Bennett, S. (2022) *Recycled Parts and Loose Parts*. https://www.thecuriosityapproach.com/blog/loose-parts-and-recycled-materials (Accessed 14/12/2022).

Huitt, W. (2009) *Self-Concept and Self-Esteem*. *Educational Psychology Interactive*. Valdosta, GA: Valdosta State University. http://www.edpsycinteractive.org/col/regsys/self.html

Jarman, E. (2013) *The Communication Friendly Spaces Approach*.

Jingna, D. U. (2012) Application of Humanism Theory in the Teaching Approach. *Higher Education of Social Science*, 3(1), 32–36. https://doi.org/10.3968/j.hess.1927024020120301.1593

Kisilevsky, B., Hains, S., Brown, C., Lee, C., Cowperthwaite, B., Stutman, S., Swansburg, M., Lee., K., Xie, X., Huang, H., Ye, H., Zhang, K. and Wang, Z. (2009) Foetal Sensitivity to Properties of Maternal Speech and Language. *Infant Behaviour Development*, 32(1), 59–71.

Lilley, I. (1967) *Friedrich Froebel, a Selection from His Writings*. Cambridge: Cambridge University Press.

Maslow, A. H. (1943) A Theory of Human Motivation. *Psychological Review*, 50, 370–96.

Maslow, A. H. (1970) *Motivation and Personality*. New York: Harper & Row Publishers.

McCormack, B. and McCance, T. (2010) *Person-Centred Nursing: Theory and Practice* (p. 325) London: Wiley Blackwell.

McCormack, B. and McCance, T. (2016) *Person-Centred Practice in Nursing and Health Care: Theory and Practice* (2nd ed.). London: Wiley Blackwell.

Miller, L. and Cable, C. (1992) *Professionalism in the Early Years*. London: Hodder Education.

Norman, A. (2022) *Historical Perspectives Ion Infant Care*. London: Bloomsbury.

Rinaldi, C. and Samson, J. (2008) Teaching Exceptional Children. English Language Learners and Response to Intervention Referral Considerations. *English Journal*, 40(5), 6–14. https://doi.org/10.1177/004005990804000501

Rogers, C. R. (1942) *Counseling and Psychotherapy: Newer Concepts in Practice*. Boston, MA: Houghton Mifflin Company.

Rogers, C. R. (1951) *Client-Centered Therapy*. Boston, MA: Hougton Mifflin.

Rogers, C. (1961) *On Becoming a Person*. Boston, MA: Houghton Mifflin.

Rogers, C. R. (1980) *A Way of Being*. Boston, MA: Houghton-Mifflin.

Rogers, C. R. and Freiberg, H. J. (1994) *Freedom to Learn*. Columbus, OH: Charles Merrill Publishing Company.

Stonehouse, A. (1989) Nice Ladies Who Love Children: The Status of the Early Childhood Professional in Society. *Early Childhood Development and Care*, 52(1–4), 61–79.

Taggart, G. (2001) Nurturing Spirituality: A Rationale for Holistic Education. *International Journal of Children's Spirituality*, 6(3), 325–339.

Taggart, G. (2004) Whitehead and Marcuse: Teaching the "art of Life". *Process Papers*, 8, 53–67.

Taggart, G. (2011) Don't We Care?: The Ethics and Emotional Labour of Early Years Professionalism. *Early Years an International Research Journal*, 31(1), 85–95. https://doi.org/10.1080/09575146.2010.536948

Taggart, G. (2015) Sustaining Care: Cultivating Mindful Practice in Early Years Professional Development. *Early Years: An International Research Journal*, 35(4), 381–393. https://doi.org/10.1080/09575146.2015.1105200

Taggart, G. (2016) Compassionate Pedagogy: The Ethics of Care in Early Childhood Professionalism. *European Early Childhood Education Research Journal*, 24(2), 173–185. https://doi.org/10.1080/1350293X.2014.970847

Taggart, G. (2019a) Cultivating Ethical Dispositions in Early Childhood Practice for an Ethic of Care: A Contemplative Approach. In R. Langford (Ed.), *Theorising Feminist Ethics of Care in Early Childhood Practice: Possibilities and Dangers* (pp. 43–58). London: Bloomsbury.

Taggart, G. (2019b) From Mothering to Social Compassion: The Ethical Context of Early Childhood Education. In G. Barton and S. Garvis (Eds.), *Learning, Teaching and Theorizing Compassion and Empathy in Education* (pp. 120–135). London: Palgrave.

Thurman, R. A. F. (1994) *Meditation and education: Buddhist India, Tibet and modern America*. https://www.contemplativemind.org/admin/wp-content/uploads/thurman.pdf (Accessed 15/04/2021).

Valentine, M. (1999) The Reggio Emilia Approach to Early Years Education. Early Education Support Series. @inproceedings. The RE Conference.

White, J. (2009) Bakhtinian Dialogism: A Philosophical and Methodological Route to Dialogue and Difference? *Annual Conference of the Philosophy of Education Society of Australasia*. https://www.researchgate.net/profile/E-White/publication/242580201_Bakhtinian_dialogism_A_philosophical_and_methodological_route_to_dialogue_and_difference/links/559a66b808ae99aa62ccb40f/Bakhtinian-dialogism-A-philosophical-and-methodological-route-to-dialogue-and-difference.pdf (Accessed 28/05/2022).

White, J. (2015) *Introducing Dialogic Pedagogy: Provocations for the Early Years*. London: Routledge.

4   Person-Centred Support

Supervision in early years practice

Introduction and Context

In recent years, reflection has become a regular feature for early years practitioners to develop their pedagogical experiences and evaluate their role and practice (Brooker, 2010, 2016). Practitioners are also frequently requested to complete reflective logs as part of their assessment and professional aspirations, specifically as a way of supporting supervision in early years centres. This chapter focuses on the value of a PCA during reflective practice, supervision as well as planning and supporting a practitioner's development. Person-centred supervision and planning emphasises the intrinsic value and motivation to successfully work together. This can be applied at differing levels with both leaders and practitioners in their roles. Tensions can exist to hide personal thinking when an individual is unsure or lacks confidence. Once these tensions are openly discussed and worked through together, a sense of identity and purpose can be achieved (Lave and Wenger, 1991) Through self-reflecting and making sense of each other as a collective practice development can be applied and shared.

Person-Centred Thinking

A person-centred approach (PCA) includes how we view, listen to, and support a person based on their strengths, abilities, aspirations and preference to make decisions to maintain a life which is meaningful to them. Person-centred thinking is therefore the foundation for action in numerous contexts and can be helpful when considering, planning, organising, understanding and connecting with communities.

PCAs include a broad range of actions at individual, organisational, systemic and community levels to support and facilitate an individual being listened to and feeling part of the early years' community. A PCA can therefore be a useful way to approach supervision with team member of early years communities.

In early years, much of the work is centred on the close relationships formed with the children they are paid to care for. Heidegger (1990) argues

DOI: 10.4324/9781003272526-5

being authentic requires us to consider such factors as the meaning of individual relationships, emotional engagement, knowledge and decision-making capacity in determining our being in the world. PCA does not provide a prescription for action but instead provides guidance towards the most appropriate approach for action based on the individual's life experience. Recognising interconnectedness of individuals' relationships can flourish. A PCA requires commitment from the persons to engage and care about how relationships with others can be accepted. Caring as a therapeutic intervention focuses on caring action so responding to an individual in a caring way suggests positive improvements with positive outcomes (McCormack and McCance, 2010: 22).

What Is Supervision?

The Tickell Review (2011) included the value of how successful supervision enables practitioners to raise their professional queries, discuss their careers, clarify their roles, support their performance management and build confidence in supporting children's development. In other caring professions, supervision is extended to focusing on ways to support practitioners within the emotional impact of their work. Elfer (2007) highlighted working with young children sometimes brings a significant emotional cost and Ward et al. (2012 in Trodd, 2016) evaluated that supervision must address emotions as a way of relieving stress and preventing burnout. It is therefore an opportunity to provide a space to solve problems as well as safeguarding children and should therefore be an intrinsic element to effective leadership. Supervision should be embedded in staff support, viewed as part of routine practice to help support and safeguarding children. While it can often be conceived as an additional meeting within an already busy day, supervision is an essential opportunity for practitioners to raise concerns about the children in their care and receive support and dealing with difficult situations. Communication can help practitioners to organise their feelings and respond to action. It can add value with children of families, promoting a high-quality service. Effective supervision can therefore ensure the implementation of policies and procedures as well as meeting settings' objectives and standards (Trodd, 2016: 439).

Hess (1980) defined supervision as interpersonal interaction with the general aim being that one person, the supervisor, meets with another, the supervisee, to make the latter more effective in helping people. Group supervision can also be a group of supervisees, with a supervisor facilitating the session.

Supervision can serve three main functions in early years practice: educative, supportive and managerial. Informed by the National Play Therapy organisation (UK), supervision within a specialist role has areas that are transferable to those working with children in early years centres. Supervision is an important part of a practitioner's role in developing their practice and reflecting on their everyday emotional work.

Early Years Centres and Supervision

- Providing regular space for the supervisee to reflect upon the content and process of their work.
- Developing an understanding about their skill set within their role as practitioner.
- Deepen and connect their thinking around child development, theory to practice.
- An opportunity to create a space to think and develop ideas.

Early Years Centres and Support in Supervision

- The support provided can include recognition and validation as a professional.
- Support the supervisee in developing key skills and expertise.
- Give space for opportunities to reflect and share constructive positive and critical feedback.
- Supervision regularly and includes the accountable for the monitoring and quality of the work being done with the children.

Early Years Centres and Managing Supervision

- Recording and having a form of contract when supervision has taken place.
- Agreement between the supervisor and supervisee regarding meeting time and location.
- A committed and mutual responsibilities to the supervision (PTUK, 2022, https://playtherapy.org.uk/clinical-supervision/).

A PCA to Supervision

PCAs are about discovering and acting on what is important to a person and what is important for them and then finding the balance between them. The process is about continual listening and learning, focusing on what is important to someone now and in their future, and acting on this. Listening is important to understand a person's capacities and choices. The principles of person-centred practice in supervision are therefore focused on listening, mutual respect and avoiding power relationships, creating opportunities for reflective actions and connecting with their everyday roles in meaningful ways (see Fig. 4.1).

Approaching Supervision: Listening

Listening in person-centred supervision involves sincere and authentic attention and intention; attention to the supervisees body language, words, meaning, inspirations and aspirations. There is an intention to understand, to know, to connect with, to make possible, to be alongside and to support a person. Listening with intention and attention is important to create

Figure 4.1 (a)–(c) Support and supervision

conditions that give voice and makes them feel heard and listened to (Hawkins and Shohet, 2007).

Approaching Supervision: A Collaboration

Person-centred supervision can support self-determination by offering ways to listen to what is important to act upon these things. PCAs challenge power balances between supervisor and supervisee. PCAs focus on working with people rather than disempowering them by doing things for or to them (Rogers, 1969, 1970) (Fig. 4.2).

Approaching Supervision: Together Teams

Listening alone is insufficient if there is not a sense of a clear intention of acting on what is heard, or the objectives are unclear. Responsive action involves clarity and action to practice because of sharing thoughts within the

Figure 4.2 Working together creates a community of practice

supervisory meetings. Support should be around helping to create a shared understanding of the person in their everyday role and how this could be enhanced (Rogers, 1969).

A Supervision Session

Supervision is not an appraisal or a buddy meeting, both regular ways early years centres communicate as a community without the children present. Appraisals are often connected to their job contract and their role, related to their job description. It includes areas such as pay and sickness as well as performance levels. Buddy meetings are often used between peers, or there may be a relational mentoring, with one being more senior to the other. These meetings are often to support each other and discuss practice. Supervision is argued to be neither of these but rather opportunities to create space for reflection and development. The navigation of the meetings is generally informed by the supervisee's observation of the supervisee in their work, with the children they supervise or support in the setting as well as their thoughts about their role. It therefore extends and is facilitated differently to that of a buddy meeting. The supervisor, a leader of practice should create an emotional and trusting space to allow the supervisee to talk about their practice in an authentic way (Norman, 2019).

Rodd (2013) evaluated that supervision is a professional responsibility of the leader within the setting to support and help practitioners to use their knowledge and skills affectively to enhance performance within their daily work. Furthermore, deepening an understanding of their professional philosophies and values she considered supervision can be complex. It can address both personal and self-development issues alongside professional and team-building issues. Effective supervision is one that will help practitioners to listen to and accept constructive feedback as well as learning to critically reflect and evaluate their own performance.

Supervision meeting is an opportunity to offer positive feedback as well as constructive criticism about their performance. It also highlights training needs and advice regarding professional development. It addresses issues in confidence and honesty when reflecting about their role. Supervision should be a reflective dialogue, and this is an ongoing process with practitioners gathering evidence through their observations and evaluating their practice within collaborative conversations. The dialogue facilitates professional learning, understanding and practice because they offer opportunities for sharing insights exchanging information constructing knowledge gaining understanding and exploring roles and responsibilities. It also reduces the isolation for practitioners by offering the time to connect about their practice and reflect on new possibilities (Rodd, 2013: 167).

Supervision should be conducted within an ethical framework of mutual respect for the parties concerned and the fundamental beliefs and values which shape early years practise the values principles and objectives of the settings should be clearly articulated within policies and their mission statement and these are grounded in an ethics of care for children their families and all practitioners working within the setting (Trodd, 2016).

Focused Question

Consider an ethical framework of work.

- *What would you include?*
- *Why is it important?*
- *How do you ensure both parties agree?*

Effective supervisors include direction for further professional development, and these include

- expertise in the knowledge and skills of professional values and attitudes relevant for the early childhood profession
- the ability to share knowledge and skills
- communication skills and responding to appropriate feedback
- involve all the teams in various ways
- monitoring practitioners' progress on a regular basis
- having confidence and receptive to new ideas
- flexible and accessible to staff in their team

Working within a PCA, the supervisor's attitude, motivation, autonomy and previous experience are all essential for the supervision sessions to be successful. Supervisors, in their role as leader, should be open, respectful and collaborative. They should be able to encourage practitioners to move beyond their own basic understanding of concepts and practices to a more sophisticated way of thinking and approaching ideas. A developing ability to analyse synthesise and evaluate is all part of becoming a reflective practitioner.

Pictures of Practice

Your pre-school has a loyal group of staff who have worked together for many years. Your role, as the leader, is to decide how best to support their ongoing professional development.

Focused Questions: Decide on Decision Making

What professional development opportunities you will encourage over the next term?

What challenges might you have to face and how would you overcome them?

New and experienced practitioners are likely to benefit from supervisors who impart information, listen to their concerns and anxieties and offer support and understanding in a private one-to-one or group. The supervisory group model is where a small group of practitioners could be at a similar stage of professional development meet with the supervisor. Alternatively, they could also be both inexperienced and experienced staff and find the model of supervision beneficial because they work in a specific room together, or with an age range. The supervision involves the objective observations of a colleague's practice, without making interferences interpretations or assumptions about their interactions and then sharing and discussing these observations together as a group. The practitioners may also contribute to the process by sharing observations they have made of children and what they have noted in their development and learning as well as reflecting on their own practice. Relationships are based on mutual trust and respect with the supervisors as leaders sharing supervisory responsibilities with the team to ensure that the group possess the necessary professional knowledge and communication skills to manage a task as well as the willingness to request outside help if a problem is identified and beyond the resources of the group (Rodd, 2013: 170).

Focused Question

How often should supervisions take place and what should this involve?
The NDNA (2022) recommends supervision is an ongoing process, but the need for meetings to discuss observations and feedback depends on your policies and the needs of the individual. Supervisions allow you to

- make sure that all children in the nursery are being supported and that there are no concerns.
- share success.
- provide support for team members around any issues or concerns.
- ensure any issues and concerns are solved or supported.
- identify any need for further support and encourage staff to identify these needs for themselves (ndna.org: n.p.).

Supervision meetings provide an opportunity for confidential information and concerns to be discussed but should not be the only avenue for this; concerns should always be raised as and when they occur.

It is generally recommended that supervision meetings should be approximately every four weeks as a guide, although this can vary. Choosing a supervisor is important as they should be one that is neither judgmental nor challenged in the role, with other agendas being brought to the meeting. The supervisor's aim is to motivate the supervisee to participate in each stage of the process, facilitating opportunities to learn together in forming valuable and constrictive relationships with meaning to develop practice and create reflective opportunities (Norman, 2019). Active listening requires the depth of knowledge, skills and understanding about early years practice to be effective. Supervisors may seek training themselves to be able to reflect on their own attitudes and abilities about supervising staff. In the meeting, they should create space as supervisor to allow the supervisee to question themselves and their ethical practices. They should be able to embrace the quietness and reflection of the session and allowing time for questions and discussion (Louis, 2020: 78).

Focused Question

As part of a supervision meeting between the senior practitioner and manager, the manager wanted to discuss how the four colleagues were working together in the infant room. There had previously been conversations about managing behaviour and responding to crying with the infants who ranged from six to fourteen months. It seemed some practitioners were struggling with the noise level and becoming stressed themselves, leaving the senior practitioner to deal with the crying and behaviour by herself. The manager wanted to discuss group care and self-soothing but also support the senior practitioner in her role in leading practice. The senior practitioner was aware of the managers' thoughts but did not want to advocate self-soothing as she believed they needed to be cuddled and responded to immediately where possible. She wanted to advocate individualised care within the group setting and encourage the practitioners to respond to the crying positively rather than getting stressed with the noise level.

Focused Questions

What are the voices of the manager, colleagues and infants telling the senior practitioner?

How could this scenario be shared and reflected on to create positive outcomes?

What creative processes could be discussed to support the infants in their care?

Working as a Collective

Mearns and Thorne (2013) evaluated that Carl Rogers (1970) proposed individuals as relational creatures, affected by their social and cultural norms. The organismic valuing process which will be affected by some of these norms and the actualising tendency may need the moderating influence of social mediation of others to develop and grow. Rogers believes that when we are surrounded by sharp criticism and judgement, individuals are forced to resort all kinds of strategies to achieve approval and positive regard for themselves. This may result in relying on external authorities for guidance as an attempt to please everyone. This may also result in unpredictable inconsistent and incongruent behaviour. This reminds me of those children from a young age to adolescence, struggling to make sense of their world and their position in it, often written off as troublesome. It also reminds me of practitioners perhaps less experienced or conscious of seeming unprofessional or apprehensive of doing the 'wrong' thing, seeking leadership approval and dependent on others rather than actively being able to work autonomously with the children in their care. By developing a space of shared communication and refection, some of these preconceptions and valuing processes can be developed.

Group supervision, according to Louis (2020), is considered a continual process of rigorous professional learning in early educations as a way of guiding and supporting developing practice. Supervision encourages reflection about daily observations while being offered opportunities to enhance development and awareness of how children learn. The purpose of supervision is to improve operational practice, focusing in on how practitioners discuss children's development and learning interesting needs as well as their relationships in a safe supportive environment (p. 62).

Supervision therefore focuses on

- Encourages listening and talking.
- Space to develop and understanding about play reasons to why children behave.
- Without opportunities available, lack of communication may result in quality care and education.
- Staff may feel less recognised and develop low morale if they are unable to process and share their experiences looking after and educating children.
- By creating space for supervision leaders and practitioners can explore difficult issues and create an atmosphere where they are able to talk, make suggestions and ask for help.
- Supervision creates and contributes towards developing trusting relationships with staff.
- Reflections to writing and observation are carried out with targeted support to provide an insight into meeting children's development.
- Supervision promotes ongoing self-understanding, self-awareness and a commitment to learning (Louis, 2020; Trodd, 2016).

By engaging in group communication, it is a humanising commitment to the deep valuable and respectful way of interacting with each other. By deep relating there develops a sense of depth, intensity and relatedness of the dialogue. Including a PCA also includes considering and discussing anxieties and reluctance in areas of their role. By being empathic together the communication is centred on the process rather than a state in entering the private world of another person's values, views and beliefs. In sharing and showing empathy, more can be understood about each other, and communities developed. By having unconditional positive regard for each other and the children they care for in a non-possessive and non-judgmental position about each other a form of professional love grows. They become more authentic in their approach as a person, with unfolding opportunities for shared dialogue.

By unfolding opportunities for shared dialogue, relational depth and quality of the relationship can be achieved.

Self-Development and Self-Awareness

Mearns and Thorne (2013) discuss the importance of cultivating a cherishing an affirming relationship with the self beyond counselling and points out that this does not happen instantaneously but can be assisted with the help of another person. Persons who can be trusted and guided with activities such as meditation, taking solitary walks and simply standing and staring at scenes of great natural beauty. In an early years setting, supervision can provide this holding space with questions such as

- What gives me most joy these days?
- When do I experience the most anxiety?
- What am I missing most?

Such specific questions can inform personal reflections in a personal journal. Keeping a personal journal can form a focus around journal writing in the same way art and craft, poetry reading novels and watching movies can all help explore self-beliefs, anxiety thoughts and feelings. Rogers suggests that as a professional, the personal journey and being congruent is central to the approach. When we are incongruent, we are not responding from our true selves and rather second-guessing the right thing to do or say. Within supervision, the aim is not to put on a facade or try to appear to be superior, expert or all-knowing, it is the unconditional positive regard to give acceptance. This includes learning and developing understanding and empathise. Empathy is often described as being able to step into the shoes of the clients and to walk around in their shoes. When this capacity is developed, the person can feel truly heard and understood. It is interesting that we often think that if we have a similar experience to that other person than empathy is easier. From a PCA, many would disagree with this because it is harder to understand a different feeing to a similar experience. It may result in triggering our own emotions, meaning we are not staying present, and it is important to recognise that no two people experience things in the same way. If we truly want to understand our supervisees' experience, we must actively listen in their narrative.

Reflecting on How Observations Were Included as Part of Supporting Supervision and Practice

Knowing how to observe can be one of the most rewarding and yet challenging aspects of practitioner's roles. Initially, those engaged in training may view observations as an add-on to their practice, with little connection to how they plan or evaluate children's development. Different techniques are also taught, and these can range from learning journeys to the pre-coded charts and free descriptions. Through regular supervision meetings, the aim could include ways of sharing experiences about observations carried out during the previous month. Reflection and discussion about what was observed between practitioners are valuable in developing knowledge and their understanding about children. This includes how practitioners could support children's development and improving communities of practice through observations. Could a PCA approach develop and enrich the observation process? Could aspects of a PCA approach be used to help actively observe without influencing children in their choices of play?

Picture of Practice

Theory to Practice: Observing as a Team within a PCA

Several years ago I delivered a project over the course of a 10-week period, with a colleague I was supervisor for, in a nursery setting (Norman, 2015: 27–30). This is an example of how observations were reflected on practice, with meaningful thinking about what was observed and any changes that could be made to the environment as well as understanding about how to support the children support and their learning. Children require practitioners to do more than just watch. They also need to also listen carefully as well, and the practitioners should be open-minded and curious about children's interests. By gaining ideas from what they have observed they are able to support children's play in learning, connecting theoretical perspectives to the play (Louis, 2020: 74) (Fig. 4.3).

The project included organising a weekly session, lasting for about half an hour. The session was called discovery play and we selected a range of equipment suited for imaginary play. We then observed using a PCA, recording what happened during the play sessions, both with the three and four-year-old children and ourselves, as practitioners, observing. The discovery play we observed had elements of heuristic play and included items that encourage filling, emptying and putting out items that have been associated with this type of play.

The sessions also included additional items, such as sensory tools, fibre optic mediums, large wooden blocks and padlock chains to extend the discovery element of how things could be used during play. As a research practitioner, I then decided on the centred approach as an approach to help with observations but wanted to ensure that my colleague and myself understood what this meant. We drew on Carl Rogers (1970) and Virginia Axline's (1947) work for guidance and, specifically, Dibs in search of self was also a source of inspiration. Their theories postulate that children are able, from a very early age, to make choices and take responsibilities in line with their age and ability. If this ability is fostered, the child becomes a happier, more fulfilled and confident person. A child who develops these attributes is then better able to grow and accept the reasonable authority of those in charge of him or her and to take initiative. Therefore, I wanted the approach to enable children to consider and acknowledge their own feelings in their play. I wanted

Figure 4.3 Open-ended resources

to let children know that it is alright to feel and encourage children to own their own feelings and, therefore, to manage and cope with feelings in a safe and constructive way. By providing a free atmosphere within safe boundaries, the adult allows the child complete freedom to express him or herself verbally, physically or with playthings. We decided that if we saw conflict we would aim to intervene when we had to explore resolutions to allow the play continuum to progress. During the session, as observers, using a PCA, we wanted to be aware of how we were sitting and how the children perceived us. Body language was crucial throughout, and our facial expressions were neutral at times rather than constantly expressing and visually directing their play. If we were approached, then questions by the children would be responded to by mirroring back and allowing the child to answer for themselves. We wanted to ensure that there was time for pauses and aimed to slow down and not rush the children. We also decided we would keep recorded notes to a minimum and to sit on the floor in a discreet part of the room (Norman, 2015: 27–30).

A PCA when observing is to be:

- non-judgemental
- non-directive
- non-interpretative (Rogers, 1970)

Using a PCA helped us learn to see and reflect on the play process. The main results drawn from our project were that children seemed to want to initiate interactions with us and were not entirely comfortable with total freedom. The children were initially unsure of how to use equipment and were asking about how they should use it and wanting to find the correct way, rather than simply exploring for its own sake. There were dominant children who wanted to control the group and the environment. Repetitive play was evident during the weeks, but greater independence grew as the weeks progressed and smaller groups formed.

The Supervision Meeting Post-Play Session: Findings

Initially, as practitioners, we assumed we knew what the child wanted or was trying to say and thus reacted too quickly. Taking time to respond, rather than immediately answering, proved more beneficial and allowed us not to lead the play. By mirroring back questions, we were still asked questions, but less frequently, and it seemed that there was confidence increased in self-exploratory play. We were then able to observe without engaging. Being conscious of our body language and facial expressions, of where we sat and how much note-taking, we made, also made us much more engaged in our surroundings and, as a result, the observations we created were more detailed in not only how the child reacted to situations and engaged in their surroundings but why they had done so.

This led us to being able to think more broadly in our planning for the individual interests and strengths the children were showing. The post-supervision session enabled me to probe the practitioner's knowledge and understanding about the children they work with as well as supporting their own professional development. It, therefore, created a space to ensure that the practitioner had growing knowledge, skills in children's learning they were caring for as well as being supported through the process. By developing the small-scale project over a period of a few weeks, the needs and abilities of the children were identified as well as the thinking about their environment, benefits and challenges. This improves not only play practice in the present but the quality of provision offered as a whole as well as supporting and contributing to the continued professional development of the practitioners working with the children (Norman, 2015; Goldschmied and Jackson, 1994).

The Value of Self-Reflection During Supervision

Reflecting on practice is not considered a new concept and many areas of work now require a reflective approach within the work cycle, through regular reviews or supervision. Typically, this means taking personal responsibility for

- Continuing professional development
- Evaluating personal experience, strengths, qualities, and skills as part of a role
- Identifying ways personal strengths can be used within a professional area

- Identifying training, practice, or informal learning in supporting personal limitations and areas that could be improved
- A way of taking responsibility for behaviour and making useful contributions

(Reed and Walker, 2015: 24)

Reflective Thinking: A Process

As early years practitioners we are continually thinking about creating exciting learning potentials for the infants we work with. This type of thinking becomes habitual, and automatic in our everyday lives. This 'way of being' and reflecting forms our professional identity. Through questioning our actions to why we think about our practice beyond and within, the merging of the two in our work setting enables a *professional artistry* to be developed, as described by Schön (1983, 1987).

Skills such as reasoning and observation enable practitioners to ensure their work is responsible and ethical. It promotes practitioners to make individual choices based on moral judgements, beyond the externally imposed. Reflection therefore can be described as a social experience between people towards a journey of developing the self and promoting individual agency. Recognising the voices from an ethical viewpoint and the development of the self is to consider the individual as an active, intentional agent, which can engage with and influence the world. An individual, therefore, has the capability of possessing reflexive self-awareness and conceiving alternative ways intrinsic to their own experiences.

Brock (2015) considered reflective practice as being a state of mind, an attitude and approach beyond curriculum planners and critical incidents. It is a pedagogical approach with stories communicated and shared between individuals. Even if the ideas shared do not result in a desired outcome, reactions still occur and aid further reflection.

Gibbs (1998) included an emotional aspect contributing to how reflection occurs in the process.

- What were the thoughts and feelings of the event reflecting on?
- What were the successes and challenges about the event or experience?
- What sense could be made of the situation?
- Could something been done differently and if so, what would this be?

If the experience of an event can be understood in the social context it occurs, then the possibility to develop future practice is possible (Hickson, 2011). Similarly, in recognising emotional learning with reflective practice, thinking about the individual process is enhanced. Subjective feelings are associated with the events, and this culminates in reflecting on the way outcomes were experienced and differing possible outcomes. Therefore, the value is not simply on experiences gained but the process of reflecting on the experiences, making connections and changing future practice from the process of reflection (Schön, 1994). Larrivee (2000) agreed that reflection is much more about the development of personal awareness through subjective interpretations and beliefs of event and situations rather than an objective procedure. For Brock (2015), it is these core values that shape and develop professional practice.

Reflection is therefore

- *A way of theorising on our actions*
- *Develops Confidence*
- *Develops an active agent in the daily routine of care*
- *Supports an agency of change*
- *Increase recognition and knowledge that empowers and improves quality*
- *Enables our vulnerability to be discussed and shared with colleagues*
- *Challenges and develops our own pedagogical thinking*
- *An advocate for children in activity evaluating multiple perspectives and development*

Reflective practice/practitioner is an increasingly familiar term when working in a caring profession, especially when it is an expected approach to practice and linked to quality improvement.

Reflect in Action

Schön (1987) evaluated professionals could 'reflect in action'. Reflecting in action requires practitioners to think spontaneously and work instinctively by drawing on similar experiences to solve problems or make necessary decisions. Schön suggested that reflection in action was prompted by unforeseen situations in daily routines, both positive and negative. It helps to reframe or look differently at knowledge in action, leading to greater understanding or maybe change.

- *Knowledge in action – more conscious of this underlying knowledge*
- *Initiative knowledge TO conscious awareness*
- *Links between theory and practice* (Norman, 2019).

Recording Reflections: Initiating the Physical Organisation of Reflecting

The collation of reflective logs can be recorded in journals, portfolios, proformas and e-portfolios and provide a helpful tracking tool to re-visit. Evidence-based practice bridges the gap between theory and practice. Being actively engaged in practice, making meaningful changes enables critical and considered multiple perspectives when making informed decisions (Hanson and Appleby, 2015).

Focused Question

What could be reflected on during supervision?

General Information

What is the context, the details, activities and outcomes if appropriate?
What observations of an individual infant or groups are included?
Reflections: What are thoughts and feelings on what happened to cover the period of supervision?

Interpretation

Theory: Connect notes, questions and thoughts to support knowledge and understanding and use the opportunity to find out more about context.

Evaluation

Identify the success of the happenings and identify any developments. This is the analysis of the effectiveness of the happenings. How has this experience improved practice?

Dewey (1910) advocated reflection as an experiential learning process. He believed individuals needed to actively develop the skills of thinking and reflecting if purposeful action was to occur, suggesting there are three natural resources in the creation of a reflective thinker: these being, curiosity, suggestion and depth. He argued that curiosity is the 'most significant and vital', and that we possess this from a young age. Rather than learning from experience, he argued individuals learn from reflecting on their experience. If reflections do not occur, there is a possibility of ongoing practices being based on predominately prejudice, outdated and uninformed ethically biased thinking, reflective action contrasting with routine action (Fig. 4.4).

In following the model, proposed planning together in supervision can help in many ways.

By adopting a person-centred planning approach, supervision meeting can be used in a variety of situations such as when you are supporting someone to plan for their short- and long-term future within a range of different life situations, for example, in education, socially or through work.

- Help people to work out what they want in their lives.
- Improved understanding about what support a person needs to pursue their dreams and aspirations.
- Help to shape and clarify contributions made from different services and agencies to ensure they are effective in helping people meet their goals.
- Bring together people who have a part to play in supporting people for joint problem-solving.

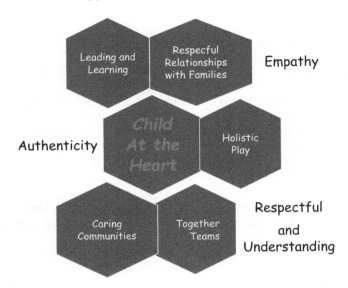

Figure 4.4 Person-centred early education practice (PEEP)

Sometimes new practitioners worry that they are not good enough. This may lead them to worrying about being critical of their practice. As a lead practitioner, I try to show them that it is ok to feel apprehensive and reflections help them stand back and evaluate the whole situation, not just their own perspective. Practice is not always perfect. Reflecting on practice creates awareness and thinking about continually improving and recognising that mistakes and unforeseen events are simply areas that can be used for future learning and improving practice. Taking the time to reflect is helpful to highlight the positive and challenges of our work.

A Person-Centred Toolkit for Practice

The Value of Process: Personalised Reflections Applying Brookfield's Lens to Practice within Supervision

Brookfield (1995) provided one approach of critically self-reflecting in developing practice which continues to be relevant in an early years contexts, caring for infants. He applied four lenses of critical reflection as a way of illuminating different aspects to teaching and one that can be also applied to early years practice, mirroring the lenses to this text in terms of infant development, theory and practice (Fig. 4.5).

Focused Question

Below is an extract from Norman (2019: 25–28) applying the reflective lens approach as an illustrated example. Read and then apply your own reflective

Figure 4.5 Authentic reflections can be risky play for us as practitioners

journey, using Brookfield's lens. Did you find the experience deepened your reflective thinking?

Infant (Student) Lens

To organise the environment, practices and support, the development we need to try and find out what is going on within the infant and their perspectives to the care and education they experience. The student lens in early years is therefore in trying to understand how the infant learns and feels in given situations. For Brookfield, it is recognising those remarks and actions we as practitioners and teachers think of as insignificant are played back but interpreted quite differently by the student.

In working with infants, I recognised this in thinking about the ethics of care and how we use our expressions and gestures alongside verbal communication in supporting the infant. How we project our own feelings and actions in the infant room, such as laughing or being unresponsive, can be interpreted by the infants as a significant signal to how they are feeling valued. It is therefore the lens that considers the power relationship and the power of the role that is given. If we assume as I purport that infants are creative autonomous agents, then they have the capacity to be critical of their care either responding verbally of physically in signalling they want to be noticed, cuddled, talked to and handled in a certain way. This lens can reveal how practice is viewed from differing perspectives. I think in working with the youngest infants it is about reflecting on the power position and how we work ethically. Recognising our authority in the relationship and what we project in supporting infants throughout the day potentially provides the capacity to reflect and interact together in everyday routines.

Co-Practitioners (Colleagues) Lens

In some ways, this encompasses positive teamwork and how as work colleagues we can support each other. This lens is about creating critical friends with work colleagues and sharing advice. *Lav and Wenger's (1991) and Rogers (1969) concepts of building communities of practice is about creating an open and honest space to share troubles and successes and for him it is therefore about listening and not just agreeing and praising each other, but also being honest and expressing stresses and anxieties too.* Sharing insights into a given situation enables colleagues to appreciate that dilemmas are not unique and by offering multiple perspectives and viewpoints cannot just solve problems but re-examine them in differing ways.

Autobiographical (Personal) Lens

In early years, this is a valuable reflective lens in listening to the voices of practitioners working in early childhood education and care. For those working with children, the stories told can often hold more value and insight to the theory surrounding them. It is the personal telling of a story that can be identified with and in some cases shape and justify the work of practitioners. *Our own personal experiences of learning, our own values and upbringing all play a significant role in how we deliver practice in the present context. How we view our own childhood and school experience with authority figures also impacts to how we react. Another layer to the relationship between infant, parents and practitioner is the emotional engagement. It is the balance and understanding of developing close relationships with infants, parents and those in paid caring roles simultaneously.*

Theoretical Lens

The final lens of critical reflection is theory and in early years there are numerous journals, texts, specialists and advisory magazines to refer to. *In my own personal journey initially engaging with readings I was drawn to* Rogers *(1969) and the way he discussed relationships in a person-centred way. At the time, I was working with vulnerable families and had been met with aggressive behaviour. I was feeling in part vulnerable but mostly inadequate in why I thought I could help in the relationships, having concerns I was expected to counsel or provide answers. It was through reading his work and applying some simple strategies I could listen to parent's complex situations from an educational and caring perspective. I went into different roles going from a diagnostic way of thinking, to observing and interpreting, moving forward and valuing the art of listening. Person-centred thinking is about allowing the space for people to find themselves rather than telling them the way to go. As a teacher of adults on a training course, it sparked an approach that gave autonomy, recognising the potential in others rather than imposing a model to conform to. By engaging in varied job roles with colleagues, parents and infants I have managed to apply Rogers' (1969) work to my relationships. In developing congruence, true to myself and accepting of my thoughts and feelings, I have been able to share these authentically. In accepting others, I have developed a positive regard and caring approach in the form of a non-possessive love. I have also been able to empathise within my work and strive to provide genuine understanding. These three areas are what Rogers (1969) beliefs essential to moving forward and for me was the theoretical underpinning of an approach I could relate to but had previously unknown about. Subsequently, this led me to develop my thinking about humanistic psychology and the subjective self. I not only developed my practice within a Froebelian philosophy, which places play central to learning, regarding the inner capacity of the infant and the value of the adult relationships. My work was skewed again when I embarked on a play therapy course. While I was fairly confident in my work as practitioner of young children, I had not appreciated how I was portrayed by the children in the relationship. By refocusing on myself within a therapeutic relationship, I found the theoretical frame critiques and modified how I approached children in their play. I learnt to listen and slow down metaphorically and literally following the guiding principles of a person-centred approach.* Critical reflection is therefore evident when contemplating a theoretical lens. It enables both the opportunity to reflect on theory itself and what resonates with one's own pedagogy alongside how theory is approached in relation to contemporary practice.

A Final Note

This chapter's central focus was in initially defining supervision how supervision could be delivered in early years centres. The latter part of the chapter then discussed examples of practice and the way supervision could be successful for development and reflection. Reflection was then focused as part of the discussion as a process to bridging the theory of a PCA with everyday practice when working with young children.

References

Axline, V. M. (1947) *Dibs in Search of Self*. New York, NY: Ballentine Books.

Brock, A. (2015) What Is Reflection and Reflective Practice? In A. Brock (Ed.), *The Early Years Reflective Practice Handbook* (pp. 7–21). Oxon: Routledge.

Brooker, L. (2010) Constructing the Triangle of Care: Power and Professionalism in Staff/Parent Relationships. *British Journal of Educational Studies*, 58(2), 181–196.

Brooker, L. (2016) Childminders, Parents and Policy: Testing the Triangle of Care. *Journal of Early Childhood Research*, 14(1), 69–83.

Brookfield, S. (1995) *Becoming a Critically Reflective Teacher*. San Francisco, CA: Jossey-Bass.

Dewey, J. (1910) *How We Think*. Boston, MA, New York, NY and Chicago, IL: D.C. Heath & Co.

Elfer, P. (2007) Infants and Young Children in Nurseries: Using Psychoanalytic Ideas to Explore Tasks and interactions. *Children and Society*, 21, 111–122.

Gibbs, G. (1998) *Learning by Doing: A Guide to Teaching and Learning Methods*. Oxford: Further Education Unit.

Goldschmied, E. and Jackson, S. (1994) *People under Three. Young Children in Day Care*. London: Routledge.

Hanson, K. and Appleby, K. (2015) Reflective Practice. In M. Reed and R. Walker (Eds.). *Early Childhood Studies: A Critical Reader* (pp. 24–3). London: Sage Publications.

Hawkins, P. and Shohet, R. (2007) *Supervision in the Helping Professions* (3rd ed.). Milton Keynes: Open University Press.

Heidegger, M. (1990) in Zimmerman, M. (1990) *Heidegger's Confrontation with Modernity: Technology, Politics, and Art (Indiana Series in the Philosophy of Technology)*. London: Indiana University Press.

Hess, A. (1980) Training Models and the Nature of Psychotherapy Supervision. In A. Hess (Ed.), *Psychotherapy Supervision: Theory, Research and Practice* (pp. 15–25). New York, NY: John Wiley.

Hickson, H. (2011) Critical Reflection: Reflecting on Learning to Be Reflective. *Reflective Practice*, 12(6), 829–839. https://doi.org/10.1080/14623943.2011.616687

Larrivee, B. (2000) Transforming Teaching Practice: Becoming the Critically Reflective Teacher. *Learning, Literacy and Culture*, 1(3), 293–306.

Lave, J. and Wenger, E. (1991) *Situated Learning: Legitimate Peripheral Participation*. Cambridge: Cambridge University Press.

Louis, S. (2020) *How to Use Work Group Supervision to Improve Early Years Practice*. London: Routledge.

McCormack, B. and McCance, T. (2010) *Person-Centred Nursing: Theory and Practice* (2nd ed.) (p. 325). London: Wiley Blackwell.

NDNA. (2022) https://ndna.org.uk/face-to-face-training/nursery-training-induction-supervision-and-appraisal/

Norman, A. (2015) Observing Discovery Play. *Early Years Educator*, 16(9), 27–30. https://www.magonlinelibrary.com/doi/pdfplus/10.12968/eyed.2015.16.9.27?casa_token=mWTzh5fvkvwAAAAA:zueTwkTxPM75wBTJo1YiITFsWN6UfYbTIwFm9z_LgFexPdV-hvOHoytX8dSXSkUeRc7OBgUfrS0

Norman, A. (2019) *Conception to Two. Development Policy and Practice*. London: Routledge.

PTUK. (2022) www.ptuk.com

Reed, M. and Walker, R. (2015) *Early Childhood Studies: A Critical Reader* (pp. 24–23). London: Sage Publications.

Rodd, J. (2013) *Leadership in Early Childhood*. London: OUP.

Rogers, C. (1969) *Freedom to Learn: A View of What Education Might Become*. Columbus, OH: Charles E. Merrill Publishing Company.

Rogers, C. (1970) *Carl Rogers on Encounter Groups*. New York, NY: Harper and Row.

Schön, D. (1983) *The Reflective Practitioner*. New York, NY: Basic Books.

Schön, D. (1987) *Educating the Reflective Practitioner*. San Francisco, CA: Jossey Bass.

Schön, D. (1994) Teaching Artistry through Reflection-in-Action. In H. Tsoukas (Ed.), *New Thinking in Organizational Behaviour* (pp. 235–249). Oxford: Butterworth-Heinemann.

Tickell, C. (2011) *The Early Years: Foundations for Life, Health and Learning.* www.gov.uk/government/uploads/system/uploads/attachment_data/file/180919/DFE-00177-2011.pdf (Accessed 15/11/2021).

Trodd, L. (2016) *The Early Years Handbook for Students and Practitioners: An Essential Guide for the Foundation Degree and Levels 4 and 5.* London: Routledge.

5 Person-Centred Planning

Teamwork and leadership in early years practice

The person-centred approach (PCA) recognises the potential in others and considers teamwork as a community with the leader assuming a facilitatory role rather than managing others. By engaging in varied job roles with colleagues, parents and children, I have successfully included Roger's PCA to professional relationships. Throughout this chapter, I will include examples about the way team and leadership styles of working could be developed within the team, the authentic self-revealed and the acceptance, personal thoughts and feelings that may correspond or differ to others. Theory and connected models will outline the approach with activities and examples also included as an opportunity to reflect on the practitioner's practice.

Why Use a Person-Centred Approach

Informed by a PCA, I have been able to develop a positive regard and caring approach when working in teams and leading groups of practitioners and teachers working with young children. I have also been able to empathise and strive to provide genuine understanding within my work. PCA also led me to develop my thinking about humanistic psychology and the subjective self. While I was confident in my work as practitioner and teacher caring and educating young children, I had not appreciated how I was portrayed by the other staff I worked with or how I made assumptions of them as a leader. By refocusing on myself within a curative relationship, I found the theoretical frame critiqued and modified how I approached teamwork. This chapter raises issues and challenges about self-reflection and teamworking, as well as leadership styles. On a personal level, it will include how I learnt to listen and slow down metaphorically and literally following the guiding principles of a PCA. Critical reflection became more evident when contemplating a theoretical lens and consider a personal pedagogy and philosophy within early years practice.

I, therefore, propose within person-centred early years organisations to include

- a committed leadership that actively instils the vision of a PCA for all
- open to continual learning about how to implement a PCA

DOI: 10.4324/9781003272526-6

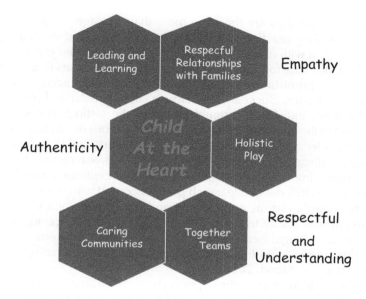

Figure 5.1 Person-centred early education practice (PEEP)

- consciously hold positive beliefs about people and the potential they are capable of
- develop equal and ethical partnerships with people
- work with people individually to meet each person's needs so that they can be in respected roles within valued settings
- promote a 'person centred culture' whereby behaviours, language, interactions as well as routines and systems and processes are all person centred (Lyon and Rogers, 1981) (Fig. 5.1).

Together Team: Teamwork and Leadership

The model I have focused on within this chapter is the together teams. I wanted to re-conceptualise the way we lead and, in many settings, manage staff, often resulting in a 'them and us' approach. In many successful and established organisations with ownership of numerous early years centres, there is not only a hierarchal system within the company but a physical divide between senior staff and those working with the children. While this could be argued to contribute to the success of centres, I argue that such a separation, with the senior team working away from the children, leads to an increased disconnection of care. Talking in confidence to many practitioners for over thirty years, there remains an aspirational idea of how the daily care meets the children by the senior staff and the quite different realities of those working daily with the children. Perhaps more regular working with the children and together as a team may build bridges and together enhance connectedness. Leaders are therefore more than managers. They are at the forefront of leading practice and modelling, critiquing and evaluating their own practice and with others in consistently aiming for better outcomes with the children they care for. Central to the success of early years together teams and therefore optimistic outcomes for children are the accomplishments of positive leadership. Success is therefore a shared vision and principles of care, education, individual comprehension of the setting's purpose and a commitment to the children they serve. There are various distinctions between the roles of leadership and management and teamwork, and I was fortunate to work with a colleague (Cottle and Alexander, 2012) teaching on a leadership module addressing these issues. We explored perceptions around various definitions. The DfES defined leadership as concerned with 'vision and influencing the future' or as the construction and preservation of a vision within a culture and the ability to work with people (Jones and Pound, 2008: 8). Management, distinguished from leadership, is often concerned with the tasks of the present including planning, organising, co-ordinating and controlling (Jones and Pound, 2008).

A flourishing team is given the opportunity to create an environment where team members can identify and solve problems on their own, delegating real power and responsibility. The team demonstrates and articulates the values of the organisation. The team seeks ways to use practitioners' interests and strengths in directly supporting the team, involved in shared decision-making and a clear vision and direction.

'A group of people co-operating with each other to work towards achieving agreed set of aims, objectives or goals while simultaneously considering the personal needs and interests of individuals' (Rodd, 2013: 149). This is how practitioners defined a team in research carried out by Rodd with Australian and English practitioners. She considered the team as being forward-looking and focused on collective goals but also being sensitive to the individual needs and interests of the individuals involved.

Whalley (2001) has also written extensively about leadership and teamwork at Pen Green in Northamptonshire. For her, 'working as a team is a process not a technique. It is rooted in an ideology of empowerment, encouraging adults ... to take control of their own lives and giving children the permission to do the same' (Whalley, 2001: 130). She defined teamwork as not only a way of looking at it as a collective group but also as a vision with leadership. It is therefore a process concerned with relationships rather than a technique following a set of guidelines. This distributed leadership model creates and embodies responsibility and leadership to be shared amongst the team. In seeking to establish a culture of listening it should have an impact on how staff work together and respect each other. This transcends to the way the team work with young children.

Katzenbach and Smith (1993 in Jones and Pound, 2008) evaluated that a team could be small number of people with complementary skills who are committed to a common purpose, approach and performance goals for which they hold themselves mutually accountable (Jones and Pound, 2008: 27).

Focused Reflective Question

Do these definitions seem strange or familiar?
  Are they dependent on context?
  Do you think some people are more accountable than others?
  Consider children, agencies, parents, leaders, local support groups and services.

Breaking Down Barriers and Building Bridges to Establish Effective Teamwork

To create a community of practice, Rodd (2013) identified that there are some key areas to consider:

- Help in reaching shared goals
- Sharing human resources and ideas
- Acknowledgement of staff professional capabilities
- Increased motivation and commitment to the task or the decision

In understanding groups further, Tuckman's (Tuckman and Jensen, 1977) group model has been described to reflect and consider the ways people come together and form a team; the process of the group individuals moving though different tensions and agreements as they take shape as a team.

Created by Tuckman (1965) and revised by Tuckman and Mary Ann Conover Jensen (Tuckman and Jensen, 1977), the group development model presents stages of forming, storming, norming, performing and adjourning. This model has a unique history in that it became popularised in academic literature. It is significant because it responded both to the growing importance of groups in the workplace and to the lack of applicable research of the time. It was valuable for practice by describing the new ways that people were working together, helping group members understand what was happening in the development process and providing leaders a way to predict the stages of growth in groups. It was useful for theory development by providing a common language and what Rickards and Moger (2000: 277) called, 'a simple means of discussing and exploring team dynamics'.

Forming

The first stage of the model the group becomes oriented to creating ground rules, meaning about the organisation and tests the boundaries for interpersonal and task behaviours. This is also the stage in which group members establish relationships with leaders, organizational standards and each other.

Storming

The second stage represents a time of intergroup conflict. This phase is characterised by lack of unity and opposition around relational issues. Group members resist moving into unknown areas of interpersonal relations and seek to retain their security. Tuckman (1965: 386) stated that the group members become hostile towards one another and towards a facilitator or leader as a means of expressing their individuality and resisting the forming of the group. In this stage, members may have an emotional response to their work, especially when work aims, and goals are associated with self-understanding and self-change. Emotional responses may be more visible in groups working in caring professions because impersonal and intellectual tasks may be secondary, although even in these occupations, resistance may still be present.

Norming

During the third phase, a cohesive group develops. Group members accept each other's idiosyncrasies and express personal opinions. Roles and norms are established. Neuman and Wright (1999) described this as a stage of developing shared mental models and discovering the most effective ways to work with each other. Tuckman (1965) stated that in this stage, the group becomes an entity as members develop in-group feeling and seek to maintain and perpetuate the group. Task conflicts are avoided to ensure harmony.

Performing

In the final stage of the original model, the group develops 'functional role relatedness' as evaluated by Tuckman (1965). The group adapt and carry out their roles that will enhance the task activities and routine of the day. Structure is supportive of task performance. Roles become flexible and functional, and group energy is directed into the task.

Adjourning

In 1977, Tuckman and Jensen reviewed the model and identified a fifth stage, 'adjourning'. This revision reflected a group life cycle model in which separation is an important issue throughout the life of the group.

To contextualise why understanding about groups of people in forming teams is important in early years centres, we need to reflect why we are there. The primary role of a practitioner is to care and educate the children in the setting, with good working relationships being fundamental to positive outcomes for children (Rodd, 2013).

In the twenty-first century, there continues to be a call for improved accessibility to qualifications, and rather than creating more flexibility to staffing ratios (2022), more investment into the sector is needed at a national level. A concern from a personal perspective, drawing on Tuckman's model, is that early years teams are susceptible to be perpetually at the forming and storming stages of group formation.

The Social Mobility Commission published a report in England (2020) and concluded that the turnover of staff was 37% of early years workers leave their employer within two years (Gov.UK, 2020).

The commission warned that this high turnover of staff impacts the quality of service offered by early years providers as well as children's outcomes. While this was 2020, the impact of the pandemic is likely to have worsened these trends and a rise in figures. Early years practitioners often have a high workload and many responsibilities. Many workers said that their work included heavy cleaning tasks, including washing windows and cleaning floors, as well as highlighting the low pay rates in the sector. Many childcare workers reported working at second jobs to help make ends meet. Early years staff were also found to work longer hours than comparable occupations, with findings that full-time early years staff could work more than 42 hours a week (Lawler, 2020).

Acknowledging and reflecting the importance of the early years sector is to address professionalisation and staffing issues. Considerations about valuing the times for teams to grow together improve retention and supporting leaders through continuous professional development, and wages are all areas that can have a lasting impact on the sector. At a local level, it could also facilitate ways of moving teams from storming to norming, to flourishing and creative teams with a sense of well-being. PCA underpins an approach at local level that values the individuals within the team, acknowledging the long-term investment in individuals to thrive. Consideration of the emotional relationship and ways of supporting new staff may be familiar to many and less to others. Two anecdotal case studies below illustrate ways a PCA has been implicitly integrated into practice within teams. Consider the principles of a PCA in reading the extracts. These include empathy, understanding and congruent (Fig. 5.2).

Pictures of Practice

Working as a Team

Case study 1

I have been a mentor to a new member of staff. I have visited her, during her first week, and completed two meetings to support her settling into a new position. She has been employed as a key person to a small group of children in the pre-school setting. We are currently making new changes to the area, changing the environment and the way we work with the children. Therefore, the new staff member has more responsibility from her previous role. During the end of the second week, an incident arose that I had to deal with. Another more experienced key person, who is working closely with her, states she had looked upset and had started crying to herself when she was supporting the children during an activity. She had been approached several minutes before by the owner who had had supported her practice. The key person asked her if she was alright. She stated yes but appeared upset. I was informed of the incident during a break.

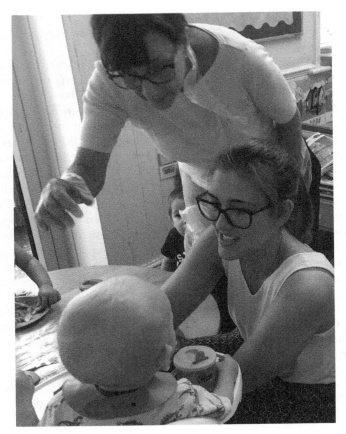

Figure 5.2 Working together

What Options Were Considered

I was initially informed about the incident by the more experienced key person, who stated when the incident occurred and how she had felt it needed to be further investigated.

I then had a general mentor meeting about how the new staff were getting on in the setting. I spoke to the new key person, individually away from the children. We looked at how she had settled in generally and drew up a mentoring plan. I discussed areas to develop and areas that were positive.

We focused on three main areas collaboratively.

1 These were emotional supporting strategies in relation to the children's emotional policy.
2 I also talked to her about how she felt with other staff members and how she was generally feeling. She also initiated discussion about her position

within the teams and her own feelings during the day, feelings of anxiety and feelings of safety.

3 We discussed the times she felt anxious or upset. She followed this up with the incident about how she needed to understand the observation schedule and the value of play and planning with the children for them to develop alongside meeting regulations.

A Person-Centred Approach to Resolution

The practitioner discussed her practices and her lack of confidence, despite being trained a few years prior. She also mentioned she had less experience with this age group. She mentioned she had been upset about being told to do something. We then discussed communication and how this could be achieved. We discussed different styles about how management is account-able to the delivery of high-quality provision and how this is cascaded down to the staff, so they felt listened to. We included on the development sheet how she could develop confidence in expressing herself and com-municate worries about practices and not to personalise them as a fault, but rather as part of professional development. I also stated, with empathy, that at times of stress she would need to remove herself from the care of the children and that another staff member could intervene, so the children are not affected.

The room has an additional member, so ratios are always exceeding recommended guidelines.

I followed this up with a meeting with the owner to discuss her worries and the development areas we had included on the mentor sheets. We discussed different ways to support the staff member and the owner agreed that she should be observed and then a meeting held weekly at the beginning rather than approaching her during her working day. The owner also expressed a need to support and develop new staff and the necessity to not personalise a minor issue as a reflection on her overall performance.

I agreed with the importance of communication, and we agreed to hold another meeting at the end of the week and to intervene less and allow her to gain skills and model other practitioners for a few days even if they would need to be discussed.

We also discussed sending the new staff on continuous professional training to gain confidence in understanding the areas of learning and the expectations expected of this age group.

What Can Be Learnt

- To gain the whole picture of a scenario and hear all perspectives rather than just one.
- To develop a good working relationship among management and staff.
- To minimize conflicting situations to support children.

- To enable staff to reflect on their practices and communication and how their own behaviour is portrayed to the children.
- To gain an understanding of how children build positive relationships with their carer when they feel secure and confident in their behaviour.
- To have a strategy that the new staff member could remove herself, so the children are not affected if they are stressed.
- To refer to the staff's employment handbook and reflect about how confidence affects working relationships.
- To feel valued and working towards a common set of goals.
- Stress reduction.
- Increased motivation.
- Minimizing conflicts.
- Clear objectives.
- A balance of roles within the team.
- Good communication with the team.
- Sense of belonging and equality of opportunity for growth and development. Set up peer observations to support new staff members (Jones and Pound, 2008; Rodd, 2013).

Pictures of Practice

Case Study 2

Lola (the leader) decided to change drink and fruit time from a traditional break in the middle of the session where all the children sat down together as a community for a drink and fruit. Instead, she introduced a 'self-service' break bar where children helped themselves from a variety of drinks and fruit left prepared on the table. Some of her staff did not like this idea and found the less organised approach to fruit time messy and frustrating. They were not keen on children taking the lead around food and were concerned it would create a waste of food culture, with children throwing away half-eaten fruits.

What Options Were Considered

When Lola went on leave for a few days, the team returned to their original way of offering drinks and fruit. When Lola returned, she wanted it to return to a rolling break approach, and between the team, there was conflict about why they had changed the system back.

A Person-Centred Approach to Resolution

Once they had met as a team and discussed what had happened, they were able to self-reflect and listen to each other. They discussed the advantages and disadvantages of both ways of working as well as what the current policies were, the theory and thinking about children voice. They also reflected on their own attitudes and feelings about children leading their own play and this led to further discussions about freedom with guidance. It also enabled the team to reflect on sustainability, food products and their role in supporting healthy choices, independence and creating an enabling environment.

It was agreed to try the rolling break time for a month and then meet again and review it, but with some minor changes such as creating opportunities for children to take responsibility for its organisation and maintenance, observing the practices around offering the fruit and drink, as well as how the team and children worked together to think about food and waste (Jones and Pound, 2008).

A Process of Practice

In denying a problem within the team exists, it reinforces the situation and does not allow the process of movement to shift. Key staff may be viewed as manipulative and therefore destructive in terms of relationships and productivity. This culminates in tension and potentially a future explosive outburst.

When a leader suppresses a problem within the team, both parties could acknowledge conflict exists but devalue its significance to them. There are acknowledgement individuals that are not happy but a continuation to continue suppressing the feelings of those involved continues (Bruce, 2012; Tovey, 2012). Power position can also exist in hierarchal teams and may be identified in numerous ways, including experience or possession of higher qualifications. Dominating conversations, interrupting, crying or non-verbal responses may be illustrated through, for example, aggressively demanding change to a rota. In the long terms, this approach will impact relationships and lower quality of provision (Jones and Pound, 2008: 41, Rodd, 2013).

'Conflict in early childhood settings is a form of interpersonal interaction where two or more people struggle or compete over claims, beliefs, values, preferences, resources, power, status or any other desire' (Rodd, 2013: 105). Recognising the team issue and then addressing it appropriately and with respect is the first step.

Person-Centred Teams

Some of the fundamental principles of person-centred planning of practice are that all the local community, specialists, leaders, practitioners, parents and children are involved in decisions about their daily life, building on their existing skills and interests, identify what support they need and provide it.

Developing person-centred teams means that managers and leaders need to involve support staff in decision-making that affects them discover the existing skills and interests of staff and see how these can be used to support children and families using the service find out what support staff need and discover the best way of providing it. This is a change in thinking about power. It is suggested that when settings operate by encouraging power relationships with staff, they typically mirror that relationship with the children they sup-port, acting as if they oversee and charge of them rather than with them. All relationships within organisations need to be based on 'power-with' rather than 'power-over'. 'Power over others is the most common and familiar form of power. People expect its use, feel uncomfortable in its absence, fear the uncertain consequences of denying it and easily fall back upon it in times of stress. However, power culminates in rights being removed and one voice dominating the relationship (McCormack and McCance, 2010).

Working Together within Early Years Pedagogies

Case Study

A nursery setting team had a practice meeting and discussed they were feeling uneasy and continuing to use food as a form of play. Two staff members were struggling financially, and some families were relying on food donations. They felt although they were using basic food materials, it was still inappropriate, so they decided to use sensory mediums instead and these included,

- clay
- mud
- sand
- water
- grass
- wood chippings

as well as material such as leaves were sourced naturally. They also decided to add water to change the medium's consistencies, whether this was hot water, lukewarm or even ice. They also decided if they wanted to make playdough with flour and salt that perhaps they could change this too. The team decided they would create opportunities for dough play, by making food such as bread, but then also being able to eat it at tea or send it home. Although the younger group, with infants, stopped using food for play, they continued to cook as well. They also helped to make pizzas and other forms of breads, scones, cakes and biscuits to take home as well as eating in a setting (Fig. 5.3a,b).

By reflecting on the materials the children were invited to talk about the origins of food, sharing food what food means to their bodies and their well-being. Cultural variations were also discussed. Reconceptualising food beyond a play medium promotes deeper shared meanings. A PCA invites a change in thinking and practice as well as their ethical position as a practitioner (Fig. 5.4).

The Value of Together Teams

As with person-centred planning, the process of developing person-centred teams begins with getting to know each other, their skills, interests and support

Figure 5.3 (a) and (b) Making scones

needs. The families and children using services should always take priority in this process. The team and leader have three important interfaces:

1 with the individuals they support
2 with the community and with the rest of the local setting. Their characteristics reflect the values and skills
3 understanding required to support people effectively, build bridges into the community, support each other and influence local setting change (McCormack and McCance, 2010).

Figure 5.4 Playing with natural mediums

Negotiation, arranging meetings to discuss the issue when there is sufficient time and beginning with a joint definition of the conflict may help. Being aware of individuals' personal feelings and perspectives is also important so concrete and mutually agreeable outcome can be met together.

Problem-solving, while like negotiation, is concerned with clarifying the problem, gathering the facts, and then generating numerous alternatives. These are then evaluated with set priorities. This is then re-evaluated and if unsuccessful can approach another perspective to the problem (Sanderson and Lepkowsky, 2014).

Mediation is when a third party with no vested interest agrees and is not pressured to offer objective feedback, focus attention on progress and the self-esteem of the team. This may be helpful for larger teams and where there have been long-term conflicts and a breakdown in communication (Rodd, 2013).

Leading a Team through a PCA Involves Leaders Who Are

- Self-aware but also know how to recognize their emotions.
- Able to emotionally hold their team.
- Be an effective communicator and clearly express their thoughts.
- Be socially aware so they can view and appreciate what is happening and give valuable feedback.
- Be able to support conflict resolution, effectively managing conflicts and offering resolution.
- Be respectful to others.
- Recognise they may need to o change and learn from their own mistakes and failures to develop.
- Active listening and celebrating feedback (Sanderson, 2022: n.p.).

Configurations of Self as a Leader

The term Configurations of Self was originally coined by British counsellor and educator David Mearns (1999: 126). Mearns describes it as several elements which form a coherent pattern generally reflective of a dimension of existence within the Self'. The theory is also sometimes known as 'the dialogical self'. Configurations of self refers to 'a number of elements which form a coherent pattern generally reflective of a dimension of existence within the Self'. While configurations of the self are considered a recent development in person-centred therapy, it has been developed from Carl Rogers' view of personality being a single organismic whole (like a circle). Concluding within the sphere of our character, we have different parts of self that we access in certain situations. This can be helpful when considering and contextualising how we were in ourselves when working as a team (Sanderson and Lepkowsky, 2014).

Picture of Practice

Reflective Activity

Draw a circle on a piece of paper. Then think back over the last 24 hours. How many people have you been and how did you feel; were you the sad self, the happy self, the child self? Draw those parts in the circle. These are the configurations of the self.

Mearns and Thorne (2000) developed this idea, suggesting that each person has multiple configurations of self, made up of 'elements which form a coherent pattern generally reflective of a dimension of existence within the Self' (p. 102). The concept of configurations about self is that various alternative personalities develop and are projected in certain circumstances. Each configuration has its own desires, needs, style and view of the world. During a typical day, a practitioner may draw on various configurations of themselves. By exploring, reflecting and examining configurations of self in a safe, in non-threatening and non-judgmental environment, the practitioner may have an increased awareness and therefore opportunity to process their feelings, thoughts and behaviours and therefore contextualising the reality and impact of how they were in given situations.

They may reflect on whether they feel happier at certain times of the day, less confident in others, anxious at the end of the day. As a leader, it is not about analysing the configurations of the practitioners' self but sharing the knowledge and supporting the practitioner by offering empathy, understanding and an authentic interest in how they feel as they choose to explore parts of themselves in their daily practice. In a sense, it is a reminder of developing and articulating how to be emotionally iterate within oneself and moving beyond how a person behaved. By reflecting on how the emotions of the inner move to the outer as a process, we are then able to think about others and the children we care for, being able to co-regulate their emotions more authentically and with understanding. It is therefore connected to Rogers' idea of conditional positive regard that a person may increase their own self-acceptance when they gain a sense of worth and understanding about themselves and others. Teamwork is about treating people as individuals, respecting their rights and developing mutual trust and understanding and developing person-centred relationships (McCormack and McCance, 2010).

Picture of Practice

Case Study: Leading a Community of Practice: Rationale and Reflections

As a lead consultant supporting teams in settings, I wanted to develop this further by considering and encouraging a grassroot teamworking experience. This was initiated and organised by the team themselves through self-allocation of roles and responsibilities. The aim is to successfully bring the team together to form positive and supportive peer relationships to enhance learning while retaining their individual voice. In early years, Rodd (2013) discussed 'Distributed leadership', whereby allocated roles are shared out to each member of a team, so they take responsibly and retain autonomy in their own position. This model of distributed leadership, therefore, seemed a positive way to develop group work and the voice of the individual, through moving sites of learning and practice.

Creating Communities of Learning

Communities of learning potentially offer the opportunities to make learning happen, by creating enhanced learning environments for practitioners in education (Wenger, 2002). Communities of learning have taken a variety of forms in further and higher education, including cohort groups, seminar dialogue groups and extra curricula activities and mentoring schemes. Visiting an exhibition at a museum and then sharing the experience afterwards seemed a good opportunity for practitioners to self-reflect about their community of learning and engagement.

Organising the Trip

By organising the trip together, communication, mutual support and the collaboration necessary for effective learning were initially discussed and explored. Practitioners were encouraged to contribute to their perspectives of feelings and anxieties visiting public places. Communication is therefore key and sharing expectations, objectives and outcomes of the visit was vital to the initial planning stages. Practitioners were encouraged to map an agreed rationale for trip success, focusing on the groups' needs and purpose of the visit itself.

The collaborative relationship of moving sites, in this instance a museum trip, to learn together also has benefits in terms of creating social support, sharing anxieties and reducing stress (Rogers, 1951). If less experienced practitioners feel supported, feelings of being listened to and valued is evident. Clough and Corbett (2000) suggest successful learning is linked to experiences and Lyon and Rogers (1981) extend this with a PCA. In being person-centred, listening, being empathic and authentic all contribute to a successful team with individuals being responded to equally.

Developing a community of practice is of course not without anxiety and tension (Garvey, 2009). Wenger believed tensions exist to hide personal thinking when an individual is unsure or lacks confidence. Planning the exhibition to visit in the museum together and discussing their concerns about physically going beyond known environments were shared together. Using the risk assessment as a starting point opened discussions about constraints. Boundaries and tensions were openly discussed and worked through. Through reflective practice, a sense of identity and engagement in certain projects can be achieved (Schon, 1983). Wenger (2002) also recognised knowledge was a key asset to building a community of learning and practice. He believed knowledge fulfilled several functions, including nodes for exchange for communities to become successful and develop. He evaluated the following themes where knowledge could enhance a sense of community:

- **Self-reflecting:** Reflecting on the trip, in its planning, visiting and plenary stages.
- **Retaining knowledge in living ways:** being aware and making sense of each other as a collective group.
- **Homes for identities:** Recognising and celebrating individual differences.

Personal Reflections About Visiting the Exhibition at the Museum

I was really worried because of COVID and wondered how busy it would be but the museum was organised really well and I felt confident

We wore masks inside (my choice) and although I do not like them on for too long it was ok and we got used to it.

Being together as a team, without the children, made me really appreciate the time spent together.

It was actually really good fun and I although I knew it was a learning place, I hadn't appreciated how inspirational it was too!

I wasn't very confident in what I was supposed to be seeing but by sharing experiences with colleagues/friends. I was able to talk about what I found valuable and what I would visit again.

I always thought museums were stuffy and boring I hadn't appreciated how much they have changed!

I enjoyed the experience of having a laugh with colleagues.

I could see how the children would benefit and by taking images we could use these with the children as learning opportunities (Norman, 2022a,b).

The Person-Centred Team: The Processes of a Team

A Development Model, suggested by Helen Sanderson (2000) of Sanderson associates, provides a positive way in not only addressing how groups form and develop but how goals can be created to support the process itself, within a PCA.

Stage 1: Why Are We Here?

This stage is about clarifying values and direction. All teams need to be clear about the values and direction of the organisation. It involves providing an opportunity to reflect and communicate about what being 'person centred' means, and what the principles and philosophy of the early years setting mean in practice. For Sanderson, working through a PCA at this stage involves thinking about the direction and values viewed as well as its purpose in supporting children, families and each other.

Stage 2: Who Are You? How Can We Support Each Other and Work Together?

During this stage, individuals identify their strengths and look at how they can work together in the team. This stage involves clarifying the support each member of the team and the team leader requires to create a person-centred team. Autonomy and the culture of the setting are considered at this stage.

This includes identifying strengths and interests alongside ways of using these to support each other.

Stage 3: What Are Our Goals?

This stage considers the individuals being supported, the roles and responsibilities and the support to each other. An effective person-centred team includes a positive attitude and values of each other. This supports planning and practice.

Stage 4: Who Does What, When and Where?

This stage focuses on the hows and whys of the team with individual reflections coming together to produce effective, nurturing and listening teams with productive outcomes.

Toolkit for Practice

The Individual within the Team: Delving Deeper into a PCA

The Johari window was developed by Luft and Ingham (1955) resonated with Sanderson's model, specifically stages 1 and 2. The Johari window is a model that could also be used to enhance the individual's perception about others. This model evokes trusting relationships that can be acquired by revealing information about the individual to others as well as learning about themself from others' feedback. Everyone is represented by the Johari model through four quadrants and each quadrant signifies personal information, feelings, motivation and whether that information is known or unknown to oneself or others in four viewpoints (Fig. 5.5).

The method of conveying and accepting feedback is interpreted in this model. Two of these quadrants represent self and the other two represent the part unknown to self but to others. The information transfers from one quadrant to the other as the result of shared trust which can be achieved through socialising and the responses received from others (Luft, 1970).

An Example of Using the Model in Practice

Sam got a job in an early years setting. Her team knew a little about her and in this context the unknown and hidden areas will be larger, and the open area will be small. As the others don't know much about her the blind spot

	Known to Self	Not known to Self
Known to others >		
Not Known to others >		

What is considered in the Johari Window?

	Known to Self	Not known to Self
Known to others >	**Open/self-area or arena –** Information about the person including attitudes, behaviour, emotions, feelings, skills, and views will be known by the person as well as by others. This is the area where communications occur.	**Blind self or blind spot –** Information about what others know in a group know about but the individual is unaware of it. Others may interpret themselves differently to that of others.
Not Known to others >	**Hidden area or façade –** Information that is known to the individuals about themselves but will be kept unknown from others. This can be any personal information which is not deliberately revealed.	**Unknown area –**Information which are unaware to the individual as well as others. This includes the information, feelings, as well as capabilities. The person will be unaware until they discover their hidden qualities and capabilities through the observation of others. Open communication is an effective way to decrease the unknown area and therefore connects to the open area, with communication being used effectively (Luft and Ingham, 1955).

Figure 5.5 What is considered in the Johari Window?

also will be smaller. Sam spent most of her free time reading or knitting in the nursery garden which was her preferred way to spend her breaks and her co-workers found her to be quiet, very shy and not very interactive, a little unsociable. In using the model together, Sam was quite surprised at the way she was perceived. As a result, would share her love of knitting with the others and created a basket of wool, crochet material and books to invite others to join her as well as only spending a portion of her break doing this. She made the effort to be chattier and more open and very quickly the team were connecting more and learning about their new co-worker. Her hidden and unknown areas became smaller and while Sam deliberately kept some of her personal life private, she did reveal other parts of herself and reflected on how she was perceived by others. The others at the nursery setting embraced Sam's creativity and she led on activities such as weaving as well as cultivating the garden further with her knowledge of plants and trees.

Reflective Question

As a team, draw the Johari Window and work with it as a part of a teamwork exercise.

Summary of a Team Beliefs and Values with a PCA

To create a values-based person-centred outlook, teams express their sense of compassion and values of care.

This could be achieved through.

- Creating situations where people identify what really matters to others throughout their daily work.
- Demonstrating physicality and readiness to engage with others through activities and using a variety of communicative activities.
- Shared decision-making about children's care and support, appreciating their rights and dignity.
- Developing relationships so autonomy grows, and practitioners can express their concerns and ideas within the team.
- Distributed leadership while trusting and respecting the sharing of information and confidentiality (McCormack and McCance, 2010; Sanderson, 2000).

End Note

This chapter invited the reader to re-evaluate how groups of people come together and work as a team. It is easy to devalue just how intense team working is within a caring profession. Working with children is a huge area and at times it can feel like working with other adults is a separate set of skills as opposed to an extension of the childcare being provided. Many practitioners are not supported or given the space to reflect on working with others and the focus is predominately on the children they are going to be working with. Certainly, as a manager for many years in a busy day nursery. I knew my own professionalism was challenged by conflicts, change of team members and miscommunication. In drawing on a PCA, it aims to offer one approach to be able to consider how a leader is challenged but also reassured of the dynamics of how a group works.

References

Bruce, T. (2012) *Early Childhood Practice: Froebel Today*. London: Sage.

Cottle, M. and Alexander, A. (2012) Quality in Early Years Settings: Government, Research and practitioners' Perspectives. *British Educational Research Journal*, 38(4), 635–654. https://doi.org/10.1080/01411926.2011.571661.

Clough, P. and Corbett, J. (2000) *Theories of Inclusive Education: A Students' Guide*. London: Sage.

Garvey, R. (2009) *Coaching and Mentoring*. London: Sage.

Gov.UK. (2020) *The Social Mobility Commission*. https://www.gov.uk/government/news/stability-of-the-early-years-workforce-in-england-report

Jones, C. and Pound, L. (2008) *Leadership and Management in the Early Years: From Principles to Practice*. Maidenhead: McGraw Hill and Education.

Lawler, R. (2020) *Childcare Workers. Early Years Alliance*. https://www.eyalliance.org.uk/news/2020/08/report-says-childcare-workers-are-%E2%80%9Cunderpaid-overworked-and-undervalued%E2%80%9D (Accessed 14/12/2022).

Lyon, H. C. Jr. and Rogers, C. R. (1981) *On Becoming a Teacher*. Columbus, OH: Merill.

Luft, J. (1970). *Group Processes; An Introduction to Group Dynamics* (2nd ed). Palo Alto, CA: National Press Books.

Luft, J. and Ingham, H. (1955) The Johari Window, a Graphic Model of Interpersonal Awareness. *Proceedings of the Western Training Laboratory in Group Development*. Los Angeles, CA: UCLA.

McCormack, B. and McCance, T. (2010) *Person-Centred Nursing: Theory and Practice* (p 325). London: Wiley-Blackwell.

Mearns, D. (1999) Person-Centred Therapy with Configurations of the self. *Counselling*, 10(2), 125–130.

Mearns, D. and Thorne, B. (2000) *Person-Centred Therapy Today: New Frontiers in Theory and Practice*. London: Sage.

Neuman, G. A. and Wright, J. (1999) Team Effectiveness: Beyond Skills and Cognitive Ability. *Journal of Applied Psychology*, 84(3), 376–389. https://doi.org/10.1037/0021-9010.84.3.376.

Norman, A. (2022a) *A Mentoring Project Early Years Educator*, 23(7), 25–27. https://www.magonlinelibrary.com/doi/abs/10.12968/eyed.2022.23.7.25. (Accessed 15/05/2022).

Norman, A. (2022b) *A Mentoring Project (Part 2) Early Years Educator*, 23(8) 23–24. https://www.magonlinelibrary.com/doi/abs/10.12968/eyed.2022.23.8.23 (Accessed 14/05/2022).

Rickards, T. and Moger, S. (2000) Creative Leadership Processes in Project Team Development: An Alternative to Tuckman's Stage Model. *British Journal of Management*, 11(4), 273–283.

Rodd, J. (2013) *Leadership in Early Childhood* (3rd ed.). Maidenhead: Open University Press.

Rogers, C. (1951) *Client-Centered Therapy*. New York, NY: Constable.

Rogers, C. (1980) in Lyon, H. C., Jr., and Rogers, C. R. (1981) *On Becoming a teacher*. Columbus, OH: Merill.

Sanderson, H. (2000) http://helensandersonassociates.co.uk/person-centred-practice/person-centred-thinking-tools/ (Accessed 14/10/2022).

Sanderson, H. (2022) *Person Centred Teams*. https://pathwaysassociates.co.uk/Archive/pcp/docs/pcteams2.pdf (Accessed 25/04/2020).

Sanderson, H. and Lepkowsky, M. (2014) *A Practical Guide to Delivering Personalisation*. London: Jessica Kingsley.

Schon, D. (1983) *The Reflective Practitioner*. Basic Books.

Tovey, H. (2012) *Bringing the Frobel Approach to Your Early Years Setting*. London: Routledge.

Tuckman, B. W. (1965) Developmental Sequence in Small Groups. *Psychological Bulletin*, 65(6), 384–399.

Tuckman, B. W. and Jensen, M. A. (1977) Stages of Small-Group Development Revisited. *Group and Organization Studies*, 2(4), 419–427.

Wenger, E. (2002) *Cultivating Communities of Practice: A Guide to Managing Knowledge*. Brighton, MA: Harvard Business School Press.

Whalley, M. (2001). Working as a Team. In G. Pugh and B. Duffy (Eds.), *Contemporary Issues in the Early Years* (3rd ed.) (pp. 125–145). London; Thousand Oaks, CA: Sage.

6   Person-Centred Thinking and Listening

Parent partnership in early years practice

Person-centred approach (PCA) is a humanistic way of working and looks at the intrinsic motivations of the individual. As practitioners, the following three core elements navigate the parent relationship and will be the thread of the chapter:

- Understanding – of a given situation and mindset
- Congruence – being open and honest in communication
- Empathy – not getting embroiled in emotions but appreciating situations and the emotions attached to them (Rogers, 1980)

This chapter focuses on how a PCA is way of discovering and acting on what is important to a person. It is about finding the balance through a process of continual listening and learning. Listening helps to inform about the parent's capacities and choices and signpost resources and services necessary for them. As previously mentioned, listening with intention as well as attention is important in creating a supportive parent relationship. This approach is about responsive action and deciding what the practitioner's professional responsibility is and together how the parents and practitioners can find solutions together. This is supported by the Children and Families Act (2014) which advocates supporting and involving families in decision-making and providing information to aid decisions in ensuring and supporting the best possible outcomes of their infants.

Developing a Relationship between Parent and Practitioner

The relationship between practitioners and parents has a significant impact on child development (Desforges and Abouchaar, 2003; Melhuish et al., 2008) and parents are viewed by the practitioner as the first primary adults the child depends on for support in their holistic development. They are the first point of reference when it comes to the child socially interacting with the world, communicating from conception. Practitioners meet parents in a variety of contexts, during and after pregnancy, perhaps in a health clinic, in a support group

DOI: 10.4324/9781003272526-7

Figure 6.1 Person-centred early education practice (PEEP)

or a social service setting. Practitioners may also meet parents when they begin deciding on infant care arrangements within early years centres, prior to birth. Therefore, collaboration can occur in a variety of ways in different contexts. What remains constant, however, is the importance of the value placed on the relationship between practitioners and parents (Gully, 2014). When it is effective and meaningful to both parties' collaboration develops and mutual respect is achieved, recognising the contribution each key agent makes towards their children's development (Baum and McMurray-Schwarz, 2004) (Fig. 6.1).

Respectful Relationships with Families: Relationships between Parents and Practitioners Working in Early Education and Care Settings

Working in partnership with parents and carers is central to the early year's foundation stage, statutory framework (DfE, 2021a) and is one of the seven key features of effective practice in DfE, 2021c). Collaboration between parents and practitioners can occur at various times and ways in supporting, advising and signposting information and reassuring parents. Open-door policy as well as scheduled meetings and event days as points of contact and arranging home visits all contribute to parent partnerships. Irrespective of the ways to engage parents' consistency and valuing the relationship between practitioners and parents in providing the best outcomes for the child during their early childhood should remain central. When partnerships are effective and meaningful to both parties' collaboration develops and mutual respect is achieved, recognising the impact each key agent participates towards their child's development (Baum and McMurray-Schwarz, 2004).

Styles of parenting approaches vary depending on their upbringing, temperament, the support around them and their environment more generally. The following forms of parenting approaches include what has been observed by other parents, known and unfamiliar alongside what they have read and been advised by professionals and parenting books. Baumrind (1971 in Rinaldia and Howeb, 2012) categorised these styles of parenting behaviours, and while this is argued to be generalised and parenting a mixture of styles, knowledge of parenting approaches can be helpful in reflecting whether they contradict, or support practitioners own parenting experiences and care pedagogies. Subsequently, change and understanding can occur between parents and practitioners.

Authoritarian parenting: this is where the parents establish the rules and expect family members to follow them without exception. Rules and boundaries are strict and there is little scope for flexibility of spontaneity. Reprimands may be used instead of consequences and there is little room for negotiation. While this is not a parenting style advocated and potentially restricting, it does resemble some parenting approaches advised by popular parenting gurus. For some 'parents to be', there is a high level of anxiety during pregnancy and certainly the infants' first two years are not without challenges. Strict bedtime routines are sought very early, even before three months of age with the need for parental sleep. Feeding approaches, a source of frustration and worry can result in associated behavioural issues that anger and frustrate the parents. As the infant develops and grows towards independence, so too does the establishment of boundaries and guidance received by parents in regulating emotionally charged behaviour for infants before they are one years. In a bid to try and regain control in the household, the parents often lean towards this type of parenting, particularly if they lack support about their concerns.

Authoritative parenting also has rules and boundaries and allowance of exceptions to the rules are given. There is flexibility in this parenting approach and while limits are set, the parent can appreciate and understand their child's perspective and emotions. Children are rewarded, and through positivity, the parenting style is relaxed and fun while maintaining routines and advocating the code and morals of how they would like their infants to be, reflecting the society they live in.

Indulgent parenting and permissive parenting can be culturally led or result from the historical backdrop to the story of how the parents became parents. For some, the success of becoming a parent may be something they relish and feel honoured to do and indulging their child becoming art of their parenting. The tension is when the indulgent parenting inhibits the healthy development of both the infant and themselves. Similarly, permissive parenting does not offer much discipline and there tends to be leniency in behaviour and outbursts. Consequences may not be apparent, and rules and boundaries are lacking. This can cause uncertainty and anxiety in young infants and children.

Routines changing may be difficult in predicting what is to occur next and seek parents to guide them (www.verywellfamily.com).

Neglectful parenting may tend to be uninvolved and often do not meet their infant's basic needs. This type of parenting may have begun prior to birth with the parent not self-managing their own health through differing reasons. If the pregnancy was unwanted or unexpected, the parents may feel unprepared and challenged in appreciating how life changing an infant and child is going to be. Lack of education or inexperience of infant development may result in neglectful parenting. Attention and nurturing can be compromised and those parents with fragile mental health may lack or be troubled by their own parenting skills or repeating questioned negative behaviour from their own infanthood.

As expected, parents do not fit into a neat, singular category and throughout pregnancy and beyond will probably experience each one at differing times, contexts and under different conditions. Communicating with parents regarding their styles of parenting can enable parents to reflect on their own practice and upbringing. Through positive interactions, parents initiate positive interactions with their child and in turn the child responds positively, developing a sense of self-worth, self-esteem and self-efficacy. Through person-centredness positive reciprocal relationships, infants learn to regulate their emotions, soothe themselves and relate to others as they navigate their own sense of self during early childhood.

Rather than considering the parenting behaviour styles, Gopnik (2016) argued parenting in modern society assumes that the 'right' parenting techniques or expertise will shape an infant into a successful adult. Shaping a product is the method of a carpenter and in referring to parenting very little empirical evidence supports this approach. Gopnik concludes that it is the small modifications in what parents do that have reliable and long-term effects on who those infants and young children will become. For her raising and caring for children is like tending a garden: it involves creating a safe, nurturing space in which innovation, adaptability and resilience can thrive. Her approach focuses on children finding their own way, even if it contradicts the parent's aspirations of them. Therefore, Gopnik's (2016) not-parenting approach, genetic variation contributes to the wide range of children's temperaments and abilities. Some infants and young children being risk-takers; others timid; some are highly focused or natural hunters. She describes a wide range of experiments showing that infants and young children learn less through "conscious and deliberate teaching" than through watching, listening and imitating.

Focused Question

Gopnik's (2017) 'carpenter' is the parent who has a preconceived idea of how the infant should turn out to be in adult life. It is according to a set of rules; if they are followed, it will be fit for purpose. The carpenter parent will raise the infant 'by the book', ignoring individuality and denying the opportunity for any experimentation in their practice, preferring to teach skills.

The 'gardener', by contrast, nurtures the infant, like a plant, in a rich, varied environment, allowing for personal growth. Some infants and young children, like dandelions, are tough and will thrive almost anywhere. Others, like orchids, need exclusive conditions. Every infant however requires 'a protected early period' when 'its needs are met in a reliable, stable and unconditional way', with 'space for mess, variability, and exploration'.

What do you consider to be the types of parents who you meet in early years and do what do they expect predominately from you when considering the two types of parents?

Reflections on the Value of Fostering Parent Relationships

Establishing two-way communications once relationships are established increases the likelihood and opportunities for parents to become more responsive to their child's social and emotional needs. This may include creating supportive home environments as a way of promoting their child's learning and development. The relationship between practitioners and parents has a significant impact on their children's development (Desforges and Abouchaar, 2003; Melhuish et al., 2008). In developing an open dialogue and sharing information with parents about their child, practitioners create personal and sensitive relationships although this can also be challenging and complex. Questions raised by parents may require medical, social support or health knowledge with referrals made. While not proposing a counselling relationship, communication and emotionally supportive relationships are significant and central aspects of the parent partnership. Working with young children often requires a practitioner to assume the role of key person and develop an emotional bond with the child, so comfort and care can be authentically offered (Louis and Betteridge, 2020). This 'personal' role of sensitivity extends from the child to their families. Key aspects of a key person's daily relationships involve being available, tuned in and consistent with the children and their families (Norman, 2019).

When a child leaves their primary carer to attend an early year's centre for the first time, it can be very distressing for both parent and infant. During the transition, both infant and parent can feel unsettled and emotional. However, a healthy attachment between infant and parent has been nurtured and established infants can be resilient in the separation, capable of building loving and trusting relationships with other carers, including practitioners when the relationship has been established (Elfer et al., 2011). Practitioners are allocated key children to look after in early years centres and act as their key person developing a caring relationship. Goldschmied and Jackson (2004) influenced by the work of Bowlby, extended his attachment theory and introduced the key person concept. She defined the role of the practitioner with primary responsibility of care for individual children, valuing the close early attachments in group care (Goldschmied and Jackson, 1994). She believed it was important for families to be supported by practitioners, using a key person approach, so close secondary attachments can be made between the infant and the practitioner. The secondary attachment can therefore influence how the infant deals and copes with changes in their life. As Dryden et al. (2005: 81) state, 'the quality of learning depends on the quality of the relationship' emphasises the importance of sensitivity, stability and consistency of care (Manning-Morton and Thorpe, 2003).

Picture of Practice

Bev, a mother, has reluctantly decided to send her baby Amy too nursery she has to return to work but is not quite emotionally ready and wants to continue breastfeeding Amy for longer than she had initially anticipated. She is angry and offensive towards the nursery staff as they tried to settle Amy in and Amy herself seems unsettled and anxious. Amy is 10 months old at the end of the trial morning the baby room supervisor sits down with Bev and allows her to talk about her feelings returning to work and sending Amy to the nursery. She is accepting of the situation as she verbalises her reasons, although it is very clear, emotionally that Bev is resisting the change. The room supervisor asks Bev how she feels and what they can do to support her. Bev mentions feeding and bringing in breast milk. The baby room supervisor at this point says Bev is more than welcome to pop in at any time during her breaks or when she can leave work for breaks and feed her baby. Her workplace is a walking distance, so it is not an issue for Bev. Bev then begins to cry and says thank you as she wasn't sure if she would be allowed to do this. Together they plan and reflect on what could work for Bev and Amy. They create and think about a space for food, storing the expressed milk. They also encourage Bev to bring in cuddle blankets from home that smells of her so Amy can snuggle and smell them to help settle her. The two connect and communicate together both begin to feel calmer and more supported. Amy is cared for by one special key person at the setting who also spends time with Bev daily.

Focused Questions

How do we connect with parents?
Can we empathise with a parent who reluctantly wants to return to work?
How can we promote bonding and attachment lead care in a group provision?

The Practitioner as a Professional: The Key Person in ECEC Settings

In England early years centres which include home-based childminders, creches, family centres, home and purpose-built day nursery settings are regulated by the education authority, following an Early Years Foundation Stage curriculum (2021). Practitioners working in these contexts are expected to be appropriately qualified and deemed suitable regarding health and safety and safeguarding risks. Higher national qualifications continue to be central to advancing the practitioner role and increased recognition of knowledge and experience continues to be raised, particularly for those working with infants. Higher level qualifications have been linked to a positive attitude towards infants and young children and their learning. Additionally, increased knowledge gained from qualifications develops more inclusive pedagogical practices and understanding of their role in enhancing appropriate attachments and positive attitudes to individualised care and learning. The practitioner, as a key person, generally has responsibilities for a small group of infants, with a vested interest, promoting an intimate relationship in each of the individual infants within the group, supporting their development and acting as the key point of contact with the infant's parents (DfE, 2021a).

Page and Elfer (2013: 19) make the distinction between key worker and key person, the latter being embedded in The Early Year's Foundation Stage Curriculum (EYFS, 2021). Other care services use the term key worker, and this often includes a liaison role between services, but responsibility for their own 'clients'. Key worker systems in early years centres such as nurseries are an organisational strategy for sharing responsibility of children and for monitoring and record keeping as an 'impersonal' role. The key person may include the above but also has an emotional bond with the child in which comfort and care are administered; a 'personal' role. The key person approach is currently a requirement in early years setting within the Early Years Foundation Stage (EYFS, 2021).

Key aspects of a key person relationship: *Stop, Look and Listen*

- Be available
- Be tuned in
- Be responsive
- Be consistent

The Ethics of Care

Taggart (2011) recognised the moral aspect of care as a practitioner, especially those working with infants in ECEC day nursery contexts. Care is conceived as being guided by the practitioners' own guiding principles (Noddings, 2002) and for Taggart greater recognition and discourses needs to be shared and challenged as part of professionalism. When the ethics of care is considered as framing the practitioner's professional role, then discourse about compassion, love and connectivity comes to the fore professionally as opposed to a role which is often viewed as domestic and personal. This chapter does not specifically draw on a singular viewpoint of ethics but rather introduces the concepts and complexity associated with care. In training programmes, Taggart (2016) argues training programmes should be including the ways compassion is visible and conceptualised in developing thinking about ethical care rather than focusing on instrumental, outcome-based and patriarchal view of female suitability that currently exist. Ethics of care certainly raises questions about the emotional involvement in paid employment as well as the complexities of care giving in forming close emotional relationships. By considering this within a PCA, we need to consider the following.

Focused Question

How do we nurture emotional relationships, while retaining a professional identity in a compassionate and loving way with the infants we care?

Recognising Professional Love

The word love has also recently gained attention in the way practitioners reflect on their experiences with the infants they care for (Page, 2017). However, as a term used professionally love is often replaced with terms such as early childhood care, affection, empathy, understanding in articulating the feelings towards a young child (Cousins, 2017). Page (2011) stated that defining love in professional roles is problematic because there is no skill set that can be applied, taught or measured although the existence of love is apparent. 'Professional Love' in Early Years Settings project used a range of methods to reveal the conceptions and practices of love, intimacy and care in early years settings. The project findings produced an 'Attachment Toolkit' and is intended to complement the safeguarding policies and procedures of any early years setting which are designed to protect infants from abuse or harm in all its forms. It included videos and examples that addressed practitioners' own feelings as an integral part of 'Professional Love'. The materials were designed and to be used as a way for practitioners to gain confidence about their professional decisions in relation to love, care and intimacy and how to determine the appropriateness of 'Professional Love' in the context of their attachment relationships with infants and young children in their own early years setting (Page, 2011).

More recently, infant-toddler professional's narratives were evaluated in relation to their professional love, attachment theory and relational ethics. Their responses revealed continuing concern about where love and intimacy should be placed alongside safeguarding protocol in non-familial pedagogical relationships. The study concluded training and guidance on care, love and intimacy was a continuing necessity on how to safely interpret these theories in their everyday practice (Page, 2017).

Without knowledge and support practitioners continue to grapple with their own emotions in their complex professional role, therefore uncertain about how to connect lovingly with the infants in their care.

Focused Questions

- *Define professional love.*
- *What concerns may there be?*
- *How do we define care and is there a difference with love?*

Familiarity, pattern and predictability of carer responses give infants and young children a sense of self. Continuity of attention from key people who know children well, who are interpreting and responding to their gestures and cues, enable children to attend to their inclinations and to play freely is known as 'tuning in' (Elfer et al., 2011). Tuning in to infants can be helpful in unexpected ways, because they often express emotions that are challenging to manage, and with the support of the key person, they can share their feelings. Tuning in can also be advantageous as a reflection tool for key persons to acknowledge infants who are less expressive and more insular in conveying their emotions (Mooney, 2010).

Reflecting on a Person-Centred Approach: Fostering Parent Relationships

By reflecting on a PCA approach, it could provide a positive way of engaging in dialogue and reducing an authoritative and often adopted advisory role, subsequently creating tensions between the professional and parent dialogical space. A PCA has often been used in nursing and developing inclusive practice within education (Rogers, 2007). Person-centred planning as an ethical approach has also been successful in working with vulnerable clients. The guiding principles of person-centred planning with parents are that

- Parents are listened to, and their views and feeling are considered
- Parents are valued partners who play an important role in making decisions
- Promote autonomy and empower parents to develop a voice
- Develop a person-centred culture and reflect to how this could be integrated in policies, attitudes and daily practices (Fig. 6.2a,b)

Parent, defined in its broadest sense, includes those cares who take the primary lead on the parenting role. As Birth to Five Matters (2021) highlights, 'Partnerships with parents can be truly effective when parents and practitioners work together to enable children to create meaningful connections to their wider world and to foster a love of learning. No parent or family should be excluded from this process. Parents must feel included, listened to and trusted within their own role supporting their child's well-being, development and learning. Each unique family must be welcomed and listened to' (Birthto5Matters.org.uk, 2021: 28). Central to this is valuing parents and carers as children's first educators and gives them the opportunity to contribute to the whole of their child's journey at the EEC setting, they attend (DfE, 2021).

Figure 6.2 (a) and (b) Supporting parents through infant massage as an instructor and early years professional

Reducing Potential Barriers to Parent Relationships

The Pre-School Learning Alliance (2017) suggested different strategies to engage families that included talking to parents and reaching out as the critically important step. As Hall (2013) suggests, both parents and teachers, practitioners want the same outcomes; they want the child to succeed. Professionals need to reach out further and connect with parents. Hall (2013) advises simple acts such as phone calls to tell a parent their child did great in an activity which could help break a barrier and let the parent know that they care.

When parents disengage, it is important to find out why this occurs and then actively listen to their views to try and understand their reasons for this. DfE (2021c) outlines the importance for parents and early years settings to have a strong and respectful partnership for children to thrive in the early years (Grenier, 2021). Recognition that language, time and confidence is often the barriers for parents to engage in the partnership process. Often a lack of clarity to ways could be overcome with familiar approaches being maintained. Kambouri-Danos et al. (2018) found practitioners perceived activity and charity events as positive ways to involve parents in their infant's learning experiences and empower parent-practitioner partnerships, but the sampled parents did not feel the same. Both practitioners and parents believed lack of physical time was the main barrier to empowering practitioner-parent partnerships. Parents also acknowledged their own lack of time or availability during the settings' opening hours rather than the practitioners' lack of time was influential.

For successful parent-practitioner relationships, there is a need for settings to consider their settings' culture regarding parent relationships and acknowledge and actively address the barriers to collaboration as a way of strengthening collaboration.

Shifting the focus from hard-to-reach parents to addressing hard-to-reach settings, it promotes reflections and refocusing on the ways communication and relationships exist between parents and practitioners.

Pictures of Practice

Martha was two years old when her mother was diagnosed with cancer. She was unaware her mother was ill, apart from her increasing tiredness and fathers more involvement. Her mother was angry about her diagnosis and the family received some support trying to prepare and manage her treatment. Within two years, she had died. The practitioners in the early years setting had little knowledge about bereavement and what to say. They spoke to a local charity known as 'Simon Says' and were provided with information and links they could share with the father. The father wanted to celebrate his partners' life and they made some special keepsakes. He was not religious and did not want the word heaven to be used or terms such as she's gone or is sleeping. Some of the other parents in the setting had been asking about the situation and the father wanted to wait a little bit before disclosing what happened to Martha's mum. He asked the staff if they could not say anything until he was ready in a few weeks' time. Together the staff and father discussed ways that had meaning for the family and discussed confidentiality as a team and ways they could support Martha in the long term as well as transitioning to school that year.

Focused Questions to Consider

- *As a practitioner, how much knowledge of specialist services is reflected upon?*
- *How are your personal views regarding loss and bereavement managed?*
- *What differences are there in relation to families' rites of passages?*
- *How do you accommodate different ideas and customs while remaining empathic towards the family and other parents in the setting?*
- *How is honesty about personal feelings and limitations to practice managed in the setting community and with co-workers?*
- *How do you support the children, family, colleagues and other parents, using a PCA?*

Reflections and Refocus: Developing a PCA Approach to Parent-Practitioner Relationships

A PCA to parent partnerships is about (re)focusing care on the parents within the relationships and ensuring their preferences, needs and values guide your professional decisions and actions. This form of caring relationship is respectful and responsive, positioning the parent at the centre of the relationship. Parent-practitioner relationships in the early years aspire to be a trustful and warm relationship so parents can flourish, evoking open and honest communications. Embracing and implementing a PCA in EEC contexts positions the parent at the centre, treated as a person first, and being involved in making decisions about their children. By adopting a PCA way of working and thinking with parents, there are fruitful opportunities for practitioner self-reflections and intrinsic motivations to how relations could be enhanced. In Parents, Early Years and Learning Project (2008), the following were considered essential for relationships to prosper in a variety of early years centres.

- Strong relationships (time allocated for practitioners to discuss and reflect on how they value parent relationships)
- Unique and inclusive parents' interest and involvement in education (this may need regular re-visiting with the turnover of parents and practitioners)
- Active involvement in family, setting and community life (this is from the outset in building a culture of inclusion and collaboration)
- Regular recognition, praise and feeling valued (practitioners need to acknowledge, value and support parents' role in their child's early learning and development and building confidence)

(www.peal.org.uk)

Everyday Interactions within a PCA Approach

PCA is a way of discovering and acting on the value of developing positive regard towards relationships. It is about finding the balance through a process of continual listening. Listening helps to inform practitioners about the parent's capacities and choices and signpost resources and services necessary for them. As previously mentioned, listening with intention as well as attention is important in creating a supportive and engaging parent relationship. This approach is about responsive action and the following three core elements of PCA to navigate and develop parent relationships include

- Understanding of a given situation and mindset
- Congruence is to be open and honest within communications
- Empathic relationship is focused on not getting embroiled in others' emotions but appreciating situations and the emotions attached to them (Rogers, 1980)

It also gives voice to the parent, so they do not feel ignored or silenced. Sharing power enables parents to work together and make choices rather than the practitioner's role being primarily informing and leading the decisions about care. Within this approach, it is about responsive action and deciding what is the practitioner's professional responsibility and in working together how the parents and practitioners can find shared solutions. This is supported by the Children and Families Act (2014) which advocated supporting and involving families in decision-making and providing information to aid decisions in ensuring and supporting the best possible outcomes of their infants.

Listening to Practitioners: Reflections on Their Relationships with Parents

Louis and Betteridge (2021) evaluated there is much on offer to learn about children and their family's culture when creating partnerships. Understanding parents' backgrounds and cultural backgrounds needs space to enable listening to occur. In understanding this further, a group of practitioners from various work backgrounds reflected on meeting parents for the first time and what they would like from partnership with parents. Parent's needs should be taken into consideration, rather than the professional versus parent position:

- Practitioners should have the time to become thoughtful agents in reflecting on their experiences, tensions and celebrations of their role. This included parent partnerships, which was often perceived as an additional and separate aspect to the children they cared for.
- Creating innovative ways to bridge the home and early years centres with practice examples shared. An example of this was the use of story sacks to extend learning and enhance communication opportunities. A parent who had recently moved brought in a sack one day with a few items she had got from home in supporting the emotional transition. The event sack – moving home was given to the child and was a resource for her to share her experiences. The parents found by collating their child's favourite things alongside photographs, pictures and associated objects they were able to express themselves through play. The parents' feedback enabled the practitioner to reflect on their own practice and introduce resources collaboratively that were more personable and connected with the family.

Kambouri-Danos (2017) found 40 per cent of the practitioners thought the focal way of involving parents in the infant's learning experiences was to have parents' meetings or face-to-face chats, although only 26 per cent of the parents agreed. Practitioners also perceived activity and charity events as positive ways to involve parents in their infant's learning experiences and empower parent-practitioner partnerships, but the sampled parents did not feel the same. However, both practitioners and parents believed lack of physical time was the main barrier to empowering practitioner-parent partnerships. Parents also acknowledged their own lack of time or availability during the settings' opening hours rather than the practitioners' lack of time was influential.

For successful parent-practitioner relationships, there is a need for settings:

- To acknowledge and actively address the barriers to collaboration, such as the changing demands on family life and the increase in demands upon practitioners.
- To strengthen enablers to collaboration, such as the use of a range of methods to facilitate communications (Kambouri-Danos, 2017).

Toolkit for Practice Listening to Practitioners: Reflections on Their Relationships with Parents

In considerations of parent relationships, a group of practitioners from various work backgrounds reflected on meeting parents for the first time and sharing the care role with myself. A pedagogy of care became apparent and was defined not only by what practitioners do in their role but what they think about their role, reflecting on their values and beliefs about what they want from the partnership with parents. These are some examples I have created to mirror their thinking.

- *I would hope I was available to build bonds with the parents I meet, reassuring them and supporting them*
- *Not only advise but someone they can talk to, listening to them and letting them know there is never a stupid question to ask*
- *I found that the relationship grows further as the parents open to me about their new pregnancy. I would also be helping the older sibling come to terms with another infant in the family.*
- *Supporting the family, including dads and grandparents*
- *Being adaptable, good communication, disseminating information and sign-posting information rather than relying on what I did when I was pregnant*
- *Support with concerns and responding sensitively to care questions without being opinionated*

A pedagogy of care was therefore developed whereby:

- The children's holistic needs were taken into consideration.
- The parent's needs were taken into consideration, rather than the professional versus parent position.
- Commitment and dedication in their roles with an authentic appreciation of the significance to the development and care of infants were evident. Karemaker et al. found that staff length of service was associated with higher quality provision for infants and young children (from birth to 30 months) in relation to listening and talking.
- Complex tasks were received and unpicked with high level of problem-solving situations received positively.
- Practitioners became thoughtful agents in reflecting on their experiences, tensions and celebrations of their role (Appleby and Andrews, 2011).

Many practitioners developing an open dialogue and sharing information with parents about their child require a personal and sensitive relationship. Some questions raised by parents may require medical or health knowledge. Practitioners sharing their own family anecdotal experiences can not only equally be reassuring but also contradictory to current guidelines and contradictory advice sought in settings. While the relationship is certainly not a counselling relationship, I believe a humanistic approach could be implemented. It could provide a positive way of engaging in dialogue without the relationship becoming too advisory and widening the professional-parent gap. A PCA has been used in many contexts, including education and person-centred planning as an ethical approach has been successful in working with vulnerable clients. In focusing on the voice of the parents, the infant and person-centred ways of working social justice and rights form part of a wider social movement. The guiding principle of person-centred planning is that

- Parents are listened to, and their views and feeling are considered
- Parents have the right to be consulted about the services they receive
- Parents are valued partners who play an important role in making things better
- To develop autonomy and empower parents
- Develop a person-centred culture, and how this is reflected in policies, attitudes and practices

End Note

Reflecting through a PCA can create relationships that have meaning to both practitioner and parents. Partnerships can be perceived as challenging, with connotations that positions practitioner as 'expert' or that practitioner's and parents are positioned from the same perspective. By focusing on parent-practitioner relationships, this implies an active connection that has the potential to flourish, pending both the practitioner and parents' willingness to engage together. In generating knowledge about PCA, this enables practitioners to reflect on their own perceptions about parents and how they could connect with understanding, authenticity and positive regard. In valuing the fostering parent relationships, the child is placed at the heart with their development and learning nurtured both in their early years centre and at home.

References

Abbott, L. and Langston, A. (2006) *Parents Matter Supporting the Birth to Three Matters Framework*. Maidenhead: Open University Press.

Appleby, K. and Andrews, M. (2011) Reflective Practice Is the Key to Quality Improvement. In M. Reed and N. Canning, *Reflective Practice in the Early Years*. London. Sage.

Baum, A. and McMurray-Schwarz, P. (2004). Preservice Teachers' Beliefs about Family Involvement: Implications for Teacher Education. *Day Care & Early Education*, 32, 57–61. 10.1023/B:ECEJ.0000039645.97144.02.

Baumrind, D. (1971) in Rinaldia, CC. and Howeb, N. (2012) Mothers' and fathers' parenting styles and associations with toddlers' externalizing, internalizing, and adaptive behaviours. *Early Infanthood Research Quarterly*, 27(2), 266–273.

Birth to Five Matters (2021) in Birth To 5 Matters – Guidance by the sector, for the sector (Accessed 01.02.2023)

Clough, P. and Corbett, J. (2001) *Theories of Inclusive Practice*. London: Sage.

Cousins, S. (2017) Practitioners' Constructions of Love in Early Childhood Education and Care. *International Journal of Early Years Education*, 25(1), 16–29. https://doi.org/10.1080/09669760.2016.1263939

Department for Education (DfE). (2021a) *Statutory Framework for the Early Years Foundation Stage*. London: DfE.

Desforges, C. and Abouchaar, A. (2003) *The Impact of Parental Involvement, Parental Support and Family Education on Pupil Achievements and Adjustment: A Literature Review*. RR433. DfES: London.

DfE. (2021b) *The Revised Early Years Foundation Stage*. London: DfE.

DfE (2021c) Development Matters in https://assets.publishing.service.gov.uk/government/uploads/system/uploads/attachment_data/file/1007446/6.7534_DfE_Development_Matters_Report_and_illustrations_web__2_.pdf (Accessed 02.09.2022).

DfE. (2021d) https://help-for-early-years-providers.education.gov.uk/get-help-to-improve-your-practice/working-in-partnership-with-parents-and-carers

Dryden, L., Forbes, R., Mukherji, P. and Pound, L. (2005) *Essential Early Years*. London: Hodder Arnold.

Elfer, P., Goldschmied, E. and Selleck, D. (2011) *Key Persons in the Nursery*. London: Fulton.

Goldschmied, E. and Jackson, S. (2004) *People Under Three, Young Children in Day Care* (2nd ed.). London: Routledge.

Gopnik, A. (2016) www.nature.com/articles/536027a. 9780374229702 9781847921611

Gopnik, A. (2017) *The Gardener and the Carpenter: What the New Science of Infant Development Tells Us about the Relationship between Parents and Children*. England: Vintage.

Grenier, J (2021) https://www.nurseryworld.co.uk/features/article/eyfs-guidance-part-5-parent-partnerships-with-respect (Accessed 14/10/2022).

Gully, T. (2014) *The Critical Years: Early Development from Conception to Five*. Northwich: Critical Publishing.

Hall, O. M. (2013) Building Relationships between Parents and Teachers. *TED Talk*. https://www.youtube.com/watch?v=kin2OdchKMQ (Accessed 18/11/2020).

http://www.froebeltrust.org.uk

http://www.nurseryworld.co.uk/nursery-world/opinion/1152266/love-love-love

https://birthto5matters.org.uk/wp-content/uploads/2021/04/Birthto5Matters-download.pdf (p. 28).

Kambouri-Danos, M., Liu, J., Pieridou, M. and Quinn, S. F. (2018) Exploring Our Practitioner and Parent Partnerships. *Eye*, *19*, 26–29.

Louis, S. and Betteridge, H. (2020) *Unconscious Bias in the Observation, Assessment and Planning Process*. https://eyfs.info/articles.html/general/unconscious-bias-in-the-observation-assessment-and-planning-process-r338/

Louis, S. and Betteridge, H. (2021). *EYFS Guidance: Part 5 – Parent Partnerships: With respect*. https://www.nurseryworld.co.uk/features/article/eyfs-guidance-part-5-parent-partnerships-with-respect (Accessed 23/05/2021).

Manning-Morton, J. (2006) The Personal Is Professional: Professionalism and the Birth to Threes Staff. *Contemporary Issues in Early Childhood*, 7, 42–52.

Manning-Morton, J. and Thorpe, M. (2003) *Key Times for Play: The First Three Years*. Maidenhead: Open University Press.

McCormack, B. and McCance, T. (2010) *Person Centred Nursing*. West Sussex: Wiley Blackwell.

Melhuish, E., Mai, B., Phan, M., Sylva, K., Sammons, P., Siraj-Blatchford, I. and Taggart, B. (2008) Effects of the Home Learning Environment and Preschool Centre Experience upon Literacy and Numeracy Development in Early Primary School. *Journal of Social Issues*, 64(1), 95–114.

Mooney, C. (2010) *Theories of attachment*. St Paul: Redleaf Press.

Noddings, N. (2002) *Starting at Home: Caring and Social Policy*. Berkeley & Los Angeles, CA: University of California Press.

Norman, A. (2019) *From Conception to Two. Development, Policy and Practice*. London: Routledge.

Page, J. (2011) Do Mothers Want Professional Carers to Love Their Babies? *Journal of Early Infanthood Research*, 1(14), 1–14. https://doi.org/10.1177/1476718X11407980.

Page, J. (2015) *Love, Love, Love*. NurseryWorld. 28.6. https://www.nurseryworld.co.uk/nursery-world/opinion/1152266/love-love-love (Accessed 14/10/2020).

Page, J. (2017) Reframing Infant-Toddler Pedagogy through a Lens of Professional Love: Exploring Narratives of Professional Practice in Early Infanthood Settings in England. *Contemporary Issues in Early Years*, 18(4), 387–399. https://journals.sagepub.com/doi/full/10.1177/1463949117742784

Page, J. and Elfer, P. (2013) The Emotional Complexity of Attachment Interactions in Nursery. *European Early Childhood Education Research Journal*. https://doi.org/10.1080/1350293X.2013.766032.

Parents, Early Years and Learning (PEAL). (2006) https://www.ncb.org.uk/sites/default/files/uploads/files/NO23%2520-%2520Activities_bookletV3.1_2014.pdf (Accessed 12/06/2023).

Parents, Early Years and Learning (PEAL). (2008) https://www.ncb.org.uk/sites/default/files/uploads/files/NO23%2520-%2520Activities_bookletV3.1_2014.pdf (Accessed 12/06/2023).

Pre-School Learning Alliance. (2017) Involving Parents in Their Children's Learning. https://www.pre-school.org.uk/involving-parents-their-children's-learning (Accessed 13/112020).

Rinaldia, C. and Howeb, N. (2012) Mothers' and fathers' Parenting Styles and Associations with toddlers' Externalizing, Internalizing, and Adaptive Behaviours. *Early Infanthood Research Quarterly*, 27(2), 266–273.

Rogers, C. (1980) *A Way of Being*. Routledge. London: Routledge.

Rogers, C. (2007) Experiencing an 'Inclusive' Education: Parents and Their Children with 'Special Educational Needs'. *British Journal of Sociology of Education*, 28(1), 55–68.

Taggart, G. (2011) Don't We Care? The Ethics and Emotional Labour of Early Years Professionalism. *Early Years: An International Journal of Research and Development*, 31(1), 85–95.

Taggart, G. (2016) Compassionate Pedagogy: The Ethics of Care in Early Childhood Professionalism. *European Early Childhood Education Research Journal*, 24(2), 173–185. https://doi.org/10.1080/1350293X.2014.970847.

7   Person-Centred Approach
An inclusive approach

A person-centred approach (PCA) places the child and their family at the heart by reflecting on what a child can do, what is important to them (now and in the future) and what support they might need to reach their potential. It is a continuous process of listening, learning and action to support the child and their family. This will be developed further with innovative ways including Arnstein (1969) and later Hart's (2008) introduction of thinking about participation and inclusion, as part of a process of professional development within a PCA. Applying a PCA includes problem solving and consideration about how the most appropriate support and resources are accessed to enable children to work towards their aspirations. The latter part of the chapter will explore how reflecting through a PCA is an opportunity to listen to what individuals want in their early years community. People are not simply placed in pre-existing settings and expected to adjust, rather the setting strives to adjust to the current families and staff organically changing and responding to current needs. Moving sites of learning is therefore discussed within a PCA and how sensitive and inclusive care can be achieved.

An Inclusive Approach

In taking an inclusive approach, PCA is a way of thinking and relating to the world and other people rather than a specific technique, tool or strategy.

It emphasises:

1 What the child wants, what is important to them and what they are good at rather than focusing on what they find hard.
2 Greater involvement of family.
3 Goals based on what a child is good at rather than their areas of need.

PCA is, therefore, a set of values, skills, behaviours and knowledge that recognises the centrality of families in the lives of children and young people. It is grounded in respect for the uniqueness of every person and family, and a commitment to partnering with families and communities to support

DOI: 10.4324/9781003272526-8

children and young people to learn, grow and thrive. It places family life, their strengths, needs and choices at the centre of planning, development, implementation and evaluation.

Being Inclusive in the Early Years Caring Community

A PCA in an early years community is about discovering and acting on what is important to a person through the process of continual listening and learning about the parent's capacities and choices as well as signposting resources and services if necessary (Fig. 7.1). Listening with intention as well as attention is important in creating a supportive relationship. It also gives voice to the parent, so they do not feel ignored or silenced. Sharing power enables parents to work together and make choices rather than the practitioner's role being that of primarily informing. Rather in this approach, it is about responsive action and deciding what is the practitioner's professional responsibility and together how the parents and practitioners can find solutions together. This is supported by the Children and Families Act (2014) which advocated supporting and involving families in decision-making and providing information to aid decisions in ensuring and supporting the best possible outcomes for their infants (Fig. 7.2).

Figure 7.1 Representations of values in the environment

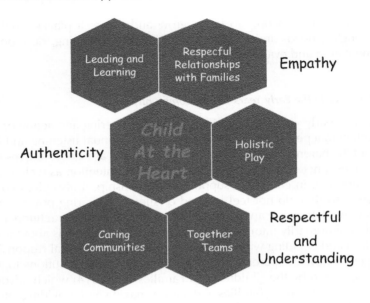

Figure 7.2 Person-centred early education practice (PEEP)

How Could a PCA Be Inclusive in Supporting Holistic Development within Early Years Settings?

It is important to collect information with a child creatively and where possible, as well as making sure the views of the child's family are listened to and incorporated into the support provided for the child. Although being person centred is an overall approach and way of thinking, there are tools which can be used to support this approach. These can include:

• One-page summary of what is important to the child and their family
• Using person-centred planning activities
• Having person-centred meetings and gaining children's views

It is important to think about how best to gain children's views so questions may include:

• Who is the best person to gain a child's views, is it their key person and parent?
• How can they be supported to express their view and could the use of symbols/pictures/objects or signing be included?
• How can we use observations as evidence to identity child preferences?
• How can we work in partnership with the family to gain the children's views as part of daily practice?

Pictures of Practice

A Case Study: The Value of Observing with Children and Families within a PCA

This is an example about how observations were used as inclusive evidence to build family relationships and identify child preferences. The children were infants and therefore pre-verbal, so the filmed observations reflected on provided a further layer of understanding them as individuals.

The project was carried out by the practitioners and the material was shared with the parents. The aim was to move away from a 'them and us' approach and encourage the practice of observations to be an active inclusive part of practice when working both with children and their families. The choice of observed activities was informed by a PCA. The activities were music time and outdoor play, and these were filmed to gain a sense of the infants' holistic development and interactions during a more structured and unstructured play session. Furthermore, the practitioners wanted to reflect on how inclusive they were in their everyday practices.

The 'Snapshot' clips of babies were filmed, and at the end of each month, the films were collated into a child's electronic personal folder. All parents were informed prior to the project and the recordings were shared. Sensitive care was taken to minimise the viewing of other babies, although at times this was unavoidable, so this was also discussed between the parents. When conflict or a child was visibly unsettled or showing signs of not wanting to be filmed, the practitioners stopped filming and supported where necessary. In this project, the focus was how beneficial the use of a micro-camcorder could be for capturing the child's voice, interaction, and behaviour within play activities. Furthermore, it was also beneficial as a way to share the filming with the parents, with the aim of feeling more included in their child's nursery. During the music session, the micro-camcorder was placed discreetly to one side on a table to capture the infant in the activity.

Reflections from the film were made, and these were particularly helpful in planning for each child's uniqueness within the DfE (2021a) curriculum supporting potential and capacity.

As a reflective tool in viewing the filmed activity, the practitioners felt the sessions were led more than they had anticipated and that the choices of songs were generally themed, with little variation. Body language of the children was noted more from the film than when observations were recorded, via pen and paper. It was also noted that disruptions and background noises impacted the sessions and consideration of ways this could be reduced in future sessions was reflected on. The giving and returning of instruments by the practitioners were also observed to be rather quick, and by providing more time and thinking space, as Rogers (1951) suggests, creates a capacity for uniqueness and individual choice.

The sharing with parents was successful, although it was noted that parents perceived their child differently in nursery during the music session to what they had expected in their experiences with their children at home. They found that their child's behaviour was interactive and positive in a peer situation. The parents were also eager to extend the songs and share them at home.

Reflections Filming Outside Play

One observation that highlighted the value of an inclusive approach and listening to the child was the filming of an infant was trying to unlock an outdoor low gate. She was with some older children who were playing the other side of the gate. The infant was able to walk and was intrigued by what was occurring on the other side of the gate rather than with her own peers, with their push-along toys. She spent time stretching and reaching for the lock, twisting, and turning the metal lever with her hands. She would turn to her peers every so often and encourage them into helping; she used language and negotiation skills throughout. She did not get frustrated but was fascinated by the mechanics of the gate and how the bolt could be turned but not opened. The gate was wooden slatted and quite low so the older children would come and chat every so often. The practitioner from the other side guided her and opened the gate and allowed her to enter their area to play and communicate. The child held the hand of the practitioner and was smiling and jumping. In response to the older children, she smiled and watched in return. Her older sibling ran over and bent down and put his arms around her and then turned and continued playing with their peers. It was not until the film was reflected on afterwards, by both the parents and practitioner, that other development was obviously occurring around the physical and inquisitive nature of the infant. These were her ability to sustain attention to what she wanted to do and have fun with the existing environment around her. The engagement of the practitioner and parent viewing the film also created a time of sharing experiences and qualities about the infant, enhancing the parent partnership bond and discussing her sibling's relationships.

Reflective Practice

Drawing on Peters (1994 in Dryden et al., 2005) data process was a helpful way of being person-centred and applying the changes that occurred using a micro-camcorder (Dryden et al., 2005: 4)

D – Describe the task that needs to be looked and possibly changed. In this area, it was re-visited that how the practitioners observed and what they felt was important in how they record. Focusing on parts of the day helped to frame and make links to existing practice and observations when informing future planning

A – Analyse the description looking at the assumptions of the time and then the responses to them. This was helpful in thinking about existing practices and how practitioners edited observations in real time without meaning. In analysing the recordings, it supported the individual capacity for uniqueness

T – Theorise a range of ways to respond to the task. By reflecting and theorising on what was observed provided a deeper understanding, in particular, making links with Rogers PCA and his theory on education and the individual

A – Act using one of the above. This was achieved by sharing the film with parents and developing observational skills in a unique way (Norman, 2015).

The overall results were the success of the self-reflections about inclusion the practitioner's discussed in their role in playing with infants, planning for play and their individual interests. The micro-camcorder also significantly increased the dialogue that occurred between parents about how they perceived their children in nursery from viewing 'snapshot' scenes. Reflections were also continually made to the differences of practitioner versus researcher in the use of micro-camcorders and the tensions between selecting versus editing snapshots included in the child's file. The project also invited further meetings and conversations with the parents and carers about the children and their play. Sharing film together encourages observations of micro-events that happened during the session, and this was helpful and insightful while organising and meeting parent sessions.

In Working with Families How Could PCA Meetings Be Planned?

Using person-centred tools and approaches can be a helpful way to gain views and think about all the strengths and positives of a child in meaningful ways, and person-centred meetings encourage the gaining of family views.

> A person-centred review is an opportunity to gather information about what is important to the person, now and for the future, what support the person needs and what is working and not working in their life.
>
> (Sanderson, 2000: n.p.)

When working with children of all abilities and inclusively it is important to plan with them and review their plans regularly. Meetings include what is important to the child and their family, from their own perspective. It is designed to be more user-friendly and informal than traditional style of meetings. There might be background music playing and circular or horseshoe organisation of chairs, rather than lots of tables which can be a physical barrier between people. The environment of the meeting depends upon what will put the family at ease and support them in expressing their views and their child's views. The aim of this approach is to be able to gather information from everyone equally. Action planning is an important part of the person-centred meeting process. It includes deciding what needs to happen to support the child in achieving their outcomes; these formed during this time should be based on what is important for the child, build on their strengths and interests and include their aspirations.

Planning the Care Together: The Triad Relationship of Child, Parent and Practitioner

Person-centred planning emphasises the importance of learning from observations and intrinsic motivations. This can be applied at differing levels to both parents and practitioners. Tensions can exist to hide personal thinking when an individual is unsure or lacks confidence. Boundaries and tensions should be openly discussed and worked through together by which a sense of identity and purpose can be achieved (Lave and Wenger, 1991). Through self-reflecting and making sense of each other as a collective, the following can be applied and shared.

- Description/What happened
- What were my feelings?
- What was positive or challenging about the experience?
- What did I learn from the experience
- What could I have done differently?
- If it happens again, what could I do?

Picture of Practice

Case Study

A dad has been attending the setting quite regularly with his son. He recently gained full custody and having spoken to the owner is keen to contribute to nursery life more. By talking to him further he asks if he could actively help in something as he feels this would benefit his own self-esteem and relationship with his son. Initially, the nursery staff were unsure how to involve him that would also benefit him, a parent with a complex family life. They talked about different areas of nursery they generally did such as the pop-in and stay type of parent activities offered. They actively listened to his ideas, allowing him the space to think and reflect about how he would like to contribute in a meaningful way. He shared that he had noticed the vegetable area looked neglected and the bush had overgrown nearby. The staff agreed, saying that they were all quite ill-equipped and uneducated in knowing how to turn it around and move forward with the area. They had lots of ideas about growing food and nurturing the area but had given up with the weather impacting on their enthusiasm. He responded by sharing his knowledge about gardening and where he could help.

Since their meeting, the parent attends weekly and is involved with all the children, in watering, digging and preparing the ground to grow vegetables.

The staff could have been dismissive of the parent but instead adopted a PCA. These included being,

- Honest about their lack of knowledge and skills within the garden growing area.
- Empathic with the dad and his dual parenting role in wanting to be an active member of the nursery community.
- Create and build a trusting relationship that the parent will be reliable and dedicated to nurturing and flourishing the garden growing area alongside the children (Fig. 7.3).

Arnstein (1969) and later Hart's (2008) introduced a hierarchical way of thinking about the inclusion and the participation of parents and how they could be involved in the planning and meeting that regularly occurs in

Figure 7.3 A willow arch was created

centres. Context and situations may determine the steps discussed, but by visualising it as a metaphorical ladder, the steps allow practitioners to adopt an inclusive approach in promoting parental partnerships and relationships.

Planner
Partner
Participant
Consulted
Represented
Considered
Informed
Absent

Absent in when the parent or family unit is physically absent, but they are talked about as a case or an issue

Informed is when information is given about care. This may include writing, leaflets, letters or face to face

Considered is referred to when judgements are made about a given situation. The consideration should be a genuine perspective of the parents although this may be subject to change. Again, the parent may not be available or unwilling to give subjective perspectives.

Represented could range from shared paperwork where the parent may not physically be available such as daily home records. Similarly, if a parent or carer cannot attend initial meetings, then perhaps a list of questions could be referred to by the other parent.

Consulted is when meetings together are held and there is an opportunity for the parents to speak and respond to decisions about care and development.

Participant is an approach whereby the parents can contribute with their own questions. They may even include their own upbringing and how their attachment issues have influenced their relationships as adults.

Partner is when the parents, carers and practitioner/s together decide when they meet what they will discuss together. It is a reciprocal process and there will be opportunities for both to share thoughts.

Planner is when the parent feels secure in critically sharing feedback about differing scenarios. They include what went well and what did not work for them. The parents may even be involved in the overall operations and routines of a setting, influencing practitioners to reflect and implement changes to routines or practices (Norman, 2019).

From Planning to Practice: Communication and Understanding with Children through a PCA

It is important to engage in meaningful talk and conversation. This means listening carefully, responding to what children say in a way which is meaningful, which invites a further response.

Supporting children to reflect on their own learning and think about their own thinking through open-ended questions help children to reflect and invite speculation and consideration. Using 'thinking' words such as wonder, remember, guess, consider, re-consider in everyday conversation help draw attention to the processes of thinking. Encouraging children's adventurous play, thinking and learning, for example, by nurturing their confidence to pursue new experiences and ideas, to 'venture' in the mind, to wonder, play with ideas, imagine, represent, speculate and make unusual combinations and connections.

Picture of Practice

A Case Study: Working with Non-Verbal Babies through an Inclusive Baby Signing Approach

As an inclusive approach baby signing can be carried out as a way of listening and interacting with non-verbal infants. Infants point and clap, and baby signing is similar. Baby signing highlights keywords that both practitioner and infant understand instantly. For example, wanting a drink and signing for milk is a clear message that can be responded to without having to spend a few minutes guessing what the infant is pointing to and getting frustrated because they want a drink but cannot be understood. Signing can enhance the understanding of what an infant wants and meet their demands authentically. Baby signing are naturally occurring gestures framed in such a way that the consistently manipulated gestures of the hand represent something meaningful, both to the infant and practitioner using them. When employing symbolic gesturing, the overall consideration is that the responses of visual cues in conjunction with sound are crucial and, with successful responses, interactions and relationships will be enhanced (Vallotton, 2009) (Fig. 7.4).

The key to successful interactional relationship is to provide an enabling and inclusive environment for practitioners and parents to create opportunities to talk and sign with infants. Playful use of sounds initiated by the infant could be a means of drawing in and involving the practitioner (Fig. 7.5).

With a PCA, the use of baby signing has a purposeful part to play in engaging with the infant's world and draws in both adults and infants (Goldin-Meadow and Singer, 2003). Baby signing slows the practitioners in their approaches and interactions, offering more eye contact with the infant. In a busy-day nursery, the practitioners may communicate unintentionally to each other over the infants' heads. Signing helps to be more mindful of this and get down at the infant's level, face them and communicate and engage with them (Norman, 2015).

The Practitioner in Facilitating Learning with Children: An Inclusive Approach in Early Years Education; the PCA Way

Self-actualisation is the education aim which is pursued by all the humanist educators, including Rogers (1951). Rogers points out that the motivation for

Figure 7.4 (a) and (b) Baby signing more and sing

Figure 7.5 Signing thank you in everyday conversations

children to learn is to satisfy their self-actualisation needs. Rogers emphasises that children should not be assumed to be passive, negative, automatic who do not care for their emotions, but rather as individuals, changing all the time within a safe psychological atmosphere. It is in the educational environment that a child can embark on their inner potentiality. Maslow (1943, 1970) also believes that the emotional communication between teacher (also termed as practitioners in early years) and children is a special interpersonal relationship, and this relationship is fostered through communication. To be effective in education, harmonious relationships between practitioners and children need to occur. The practitioner should have genuine emotions and be able to express brief, understanding and unconditional care and respect for the children they educate in relation to their emotional health. In this way, the relationship between practitioners and children can be harmonious and this kind of relationship can satisfy the children's desire for care, promoting them to learn happily and actively, imaginative and creative (Fig. 7.6a–e).

Figure 7.6 (a)–(e) Working together through mindfulness and yoga, listening to our bodies and minds

Working in a PCA connections with the children need to have,

- Genuineness, both practitioner and children should treat each other genuinely. Both should express their emotion directly and authentically. Only in this way can children develop emotional literacy and obtain real awareness and understanding to others.
- Acceptance of the child's fear and hesitation when they meet new problems, as well acceptance when the child is satisfied in achieving their aim.

Rogers (1953) believed the teacher's (or as we have defined the practitioner) task is not to teach the children how to learn but to offer learning methods, and enable the children to learn by themselves. The practitioner should consider themselves as facilitator, an approach perhaps more familiar in early years than in traditional school contexts. For Rogers, the approach has the potential to temper the psychological intense atmosphere and enable children to apply their potential. In Rogers' view, student-centredness is the same as being client-centred in a hospital. The practitioner should seek the children's trust like the way doctor treats their patients.

Picture of Practice

Case Study: An Example of a PCA Practice in a School Context in Nature

When I visited a primary school, with the reception children aged four years, I spoke to the children as a group. In the setting, we chatted about my unfamiliarity with their outside space and if they could take me on journey in groups outside and show me where they played. Within the smaller groups, an electronic tablet was given to them in pairs. I said that they could take images or film their journey with me. This was an active way of allowing children to dictate what they wanted to record and reveal.

An Inclusive Journey (Tour)

The Mosaic approach has been described by Clark et al. (2005) as a multi-modal way to listen to children and understand their world by putting pieces of evidence such as observations, child conferencing, children's use of cameras and tours and mapping together. This evaluation tool places children at the centre and has a core belief to the idea that they are the most knowledgeable experts of their own lives. For me, it was important to begin giving children agency to contribute and have an impact on their daily life experiences. It is a PCA, enabling understanding, authenticity and empathy to develop as we journey together.

The Walk

We walked down the path, and the children were very vocal and excited in my presence as a visitor. They asked what they should film, and I said it was their decision. Many children ran off with their tablets, while others wanted to stay and talk to me. The children were observed as respecting the holding and paired ownership of the tablet they were given. Numerous images were taken as the children entered the nature aspects of the outdoors. Their spoken language included,

- look at this
- look at the leaves
- see the moving rocks
- look mushrooms
- oh my goodness bugs
- wow the birds!

as they embarked on their journey. This was consistent the whole way around. The children were excitable, and it felt quite a rushed experience and initially the pace was quicker than anticipated, although slowed as we spent time outside. I was also trying to monitor my own voice and not keep inviting them to see things, rather wait for them to invite me to view things such as a robin they wanted to talk about. The children used their sensory experiences of feel, smell and listening alongside taking images and film.

The photographic images revealed a sense of agency:

- Children captured their environment via zooming in on areas
- Taking images of parts of their findings rather than the whole
- Colour and contrast were visible with man-made and nature items in their environment
- The children took images from different positions, but many were at eye level
- An understanding of depth perception and visual perception

When we returned from the nature walk, I uploaded the images, and, with the children, was able to make sense of them together. The children talked about what their images and although the walk was a familiar area to them, showing 'an outsider' their space seemed to be a novel approach for them. They were inviting and excited to be given the autonomy of an electronic tablet to take images and film of their outdoor walk. The images reflected this and included special areas of interests such as bark, leaves, corners found and wildlife such as ants. The children worked well together and did not take many images of each other, preferring to take images of close-up things on their walk. I noted the images were a reminder of the difference in how they view it. Their height significantly changed their perception, and at eye level, I would not be viewing the same thing so, therefore, missed quite a lot of their outdoor walk experience. I looked 'down' a lot too rather than horizontal at what they were showing me and again this distorted my view (Fig. 7.7a–d).

Figure 7.7 (a)–(d) Children's images of the environment

Focused Question

Was the walk inclusive and were there features of a PCA?

The time spent on the nature walk was a little restricted because of the educational settings routine, and therefore flexibility was limited. I evaluated that it was initially very fast paced but slowed down with increased time spent outside. It also took the children, not all, but some, to walk off down the path and then return to calm and assimilate their environment, thinking and reflecting on want they would like to capture it through imagery (Bruce, 2012). The time allowance reduced the fast and numerous images initially taken that had less meaning than the latter ones (Norman, 2022b) (Fig. 7.8).

Figure 7.8 Map of the experience

A PCA in the Early Educational Context: Relationship between Teachers and Children

Humanistic psychologists consider not only the children's individual differences and self-concepts, but also the relationship between practitioner, parents and children and the classroom atmosphere (Stefaroi, 2012). This includes how the practitioner thinks about the interpersonal emotion and relation, self-concept and self-respect and continuance of learning with the children in their care. It promotes practitioners to understand themselves and the meaning about their teaching styles and how they facilitate play and their attitude. The emotional relationship promotes the practitioner to care for the child's inner thought and treat and value them. It encourages the child to discover their own learning approaches and have an active learning motivation; all of these are helpful for them to learn. In moving sites of learning for young children, the possibilities are endless. Navigated by inclusive and responsive practitioners' activities such as going for a walk outside with the child in a pushchair can be a learning experience and moves towards what is considered a value-based approach (Fig. 7.9).

The values at the centre of a PCA are represented through the setting's philosophy which contains key humanistic ideas of empathy genuineness and unconditional positive regard. Rogers' learning is facilitated when practitioners employ empathy, genuineness and unconditional positive regard. These

Figure 7.9 Collaborative learning

three conditions are necessary for the creation of relationships and support and facilitate interactions. A value-based approach is a process of creating caring and learning environments, mindful of global issues and sensitive to the micro as well as macro-society values beliefs and cultures. By accepting a polyphonic and unified space, we are then able to move away from reductionist approaches to knowing. This culminates to an objective understanding of the ambiguous and contested spaces the early years community inhabit in and beyond their setting. Much of the experience of learning occurs from a negotiated dialogical space to facilitate value-based community of learning and practice. As an educator and teacher, Bakhtin's approach to language was shared with his colleague Voloshinov (1895–1936) (White, 2016). It highlighted language as taking place in social contexts that are laden with meanings, further captured in the theory of dialogism. Though Bakhtin did not specifically focus on early years development, he did refer to the role of language in a young child's life, and for me, this connects to the emotional communication and the way language is interpreted (White, 2016). Language is the way a child begins to view themselves and their personality. Language is therefore a lifelong journey of ideological becoming rather than transmitting language as a purpose for learning codes. It provides an interpretation of language that invites consideration of a dialogue as a living event and fluid in its use of interactions. Leaders are therefore implicated in this conceptualisation keeping others as the central source, rather than leading the dialogue themselves (Vice, 1997).

Reflective Question

Consider how you would create an event that involved all practitioners, parents and children. How would you develop a community of practice and ensure everyone is listened to? How do you consider what is not said as much as what is said by others?

A Person-Centred Toolkit for Practice

An example of inclusive practice is the way we engage with the outdoors, beyond the setting, therefore moving sites of learning within a PCA. Outings within the local community can provide children with enriching and inclusive learning experiences. These first-hand experiences can support the activities in the setting and make a real difference to the setting's programme. The importance of providing these opportunities for children to learn outside the setting is recognised by the Early Years Foundation Stage Curriculum in England (2021), which requires that settings with no outside provision and plan for daily outings. There are many places to take young children, from a simple walk in the local park to collect leaves. Going out can be accompanied with parents and generally is a free experience that is nurturing and part of healthy play. The natural landscape has a constantly changing nature, some degree of disorder, a diversity of living and non-living objects and a range of found components that provide endless possibilities for play, interaction, exploration, discovery and creativity (Fig. 7.10a,b).

Ernst (2014) found that the open-endedness of natural materials (materials where there is more than one single "right" way to use them) allows them to be used in many creative ways and in a variety of imaginative play scenarios, even with very young children. While playing outside, I would like the children to think about what they could do rather than what they ought

Figure 7.10 (a) and (b) Learning about coastal play and feeding the crabs

to be doing. In a complex modern and digital society, the child's grasp of meaning, at least beyond infancy, benefits from the help of adults, including parents and grandparents at home, as well as being supported by practitioners in centres (Trevarthen, 2012). Going for walks can build upon the work of attachment-led parenting (Bowlby 1969) with contemporary research supporting parent and infant connectivity, including Zeedyk (2000–2019) and Trevarthen (2000) with a PCA. Furthermore, Louv (2005/7) Nature Deficit Disorder and Karsten highlighted the rationale for fresh air, with contemporary concerns of children's engagement with the outdoors. Simply taking out a child in a buggy can experience the fresh air and bonding experience. The impact of buggy orientation on parent-infant interaction and infant stress was studied by Zeedyk in collaboration with the National Literacy Trust. When mothers were asked to talk about the two journeys using forward and front-facing buggies, they were aware of different styles of interacting between themselves and their infants. They were surprised by how much there was change in orientation when their infant faced them in the buggy had enhanced their communication. Blaiklock's study (2013) also investigated the frequency of parent-child interactions that occur when parents accompany young children in buggies while moving between shops. They found minimal levels of interaction were observed between parents and children under two years when infants were transported in buggies, facing forward and could not see their parents, because interaction was more difficult to achieve. Being able to face towards parents increased language interactions. Therefore, sensitive care, in this example, selecting buggies that parents and carers face can reduce an anticipated stressful experience and buffer cortisol surge. The small but significant changes in daily life in creating a PCA towards inclusive care.

A Final Note

This chapter provides numerous examples of inclusive care to illustrate how a PCA connects already to high-quality practice and reflective thinking. The chapter began with a consideration of parents and the way centres could develop inclusive relationships. It then proceeds by reflecting on the children themselves and, with the examples given, aims to ignite further considerations of practitioner's practices and how this could be further developed to include a PCA.

References

Arnstein, R. (1969) A Ladder of Citizen Participation. *Journal of the American Institute of Planner*, 35, 421.6–421.22.
Bruce, T. (Ed.). (2012) *Early Childhood Practice: Froebel Today*. London: Sage.
Blaiklock, K. (2013). What are children learning in early childhood education in New Zealand? *Australasian Journal of Early Childhood*. 38, 2: 51–56. Australasian journal of early childhood. 38. 51–56. 10.1177/183693911303800207.

Bowlby J. (1969) Attachment. Attachment and loss: Vol. 1. Loss. New York: Basic Books.

Clark, A., Trine, A. and Moss, P. (2005) *Beyond Listening*. Bristol: Policy Press.

DfE, (2021a) Early Years foundation Statutory guidance. https://assets.publishing. service.gov.uk/government/uploads/system/uploads/attachment_data/file/974907/ EYFS_framework_-_March_2021.pdf (Accessed 12/06/2023).

Dryden, L., Forbes, R., Mukherji, P. and Pound, L. (2005) *Essential Early Years*. London: Hodder Arnold.

Ernst, J. (2014) Early childhood educators' use of natural outdoor settings as learning environments: an exploratory study of beliefs, practices, and barriers, Environmental Education Research, 20:6, 735–752, DOI: 10.1080/13504622.2013.833596

Goldin-Meadow, S., & Singer, M.A. (2003). From children's hands to adults' ears: Gesture's role in teaching and learning. *Developmental Psychology*, 39, 509–520.

Hart, R. (2008) Stepping Back from 'The Ladder': Reflections on a Model of Participatory Work with Infantren. In A. Reid, B. Jensen, J Nikel and V. Simovska (Eds.), *Participation and Learning*. London: Springer.

http://www.froebeltrust.org.uk

Lave, J. and Wenger, E. (1991) Situated learning: Legitimate peripheral participation. Cambridge: Cambridge University Press.

Louv, R. (2005) *Last Child in the Woods: Saving Out Children from Nature-Deficit Disorder*. Chapel Hill, NC: Algonquin Books of Chapel Hill.

Maslow, A. H. (1943) A Theory of Human Motivation. *Psychological Review*, 50, 370–96.

Maslow, A. H. (1970) *Motivation and Personality*. New York, NY: Harper & Row Publishers.

Norman, A. (2015) Focusing on the Details. *Early Years Educator*, 17(4), 28–30.

Norman, A. (2022a) Narratives through Nature *Early Years Educator*, 23(8).

Norman, A. (2022b) Narratives through Nature *Early Years Educator*, 23(9).

Rogers, C. R. (1951) *Client-Centered Therapy*. Boston, MA: Hougton Mifflin.

Sanderson, H. (2000) http://helensandersonassociates.co.uk/person-centred-practice/ person-centred-thinking-tools/ (Accessed 14/10/2022).

Stefaroi, P. (2012) *The Humanistic Approach*. London: Community Development.

Trevarthen, C. (2000) Musicality and the intrinsic motive pulse: evidence from human psychobiology and infant communication. Musicale Scientia. 155–215.

Vice, S. (1997) *Introducing Bakhtin*. Manchester: Manchester University Press.

Trevarthen, C. (2012) Finding a place with meaning in a busy human world: how does the story begin, and who helps? *European Early Childhood Education Research Journal*. 20(3) 303–312.

Vallotton, C. (2009) Do infants influence their quality of care? Infants' communicative gestures predict caregivers' responsiveness. *Infant Behavior and Development*, 32, 351–365.

White, E. J. (2016) *Introducing Dialogic Pedagogy: Provocations for the Early Years*. London: Routledge.

8   An End Note of Theory to Practice

Introduction

This chapter aims to bridge the previous chapters, with some examples of practice being included to highlight how the person-centred approach (PCA) model
could be referred to when reflecting about the ways of working with children.
A PCA is an established counselling perspective having been introduced since
the mid-twentieth century. More recently, PCA has also been researched and
implemented as a way of working within the nursing profession in a bid to reflect about the care offered within a profession, governed by a medical model of
treatment. Similarly, local authorities have also included PCA as a way of working with individuals with special educational needs. The aim here is to ensure all
members of the community remain a valued member of the society and retain a
voice to be listened. The objectives, in both services, are to shift the focus so that
the individual has a say in their own care as an autonomous person.

This book invites a timely reflection on how a PCA could be implemented
within early years services and bridge practices as well as theories to support
the well-being of the child.

The Value of Working with a PCA

The PCA underpins principles of practice and offers a timely way to re-think
and re-visit how practitioners approach their own practices and interactions
with others.

The key features of a PCA are:

- the individual (person) is at the centre
- family members and those involved in a child's care are full partners,
  actively involved
- planning for the child reflects their capacities, what is important to them,
  as well as the support needed to develop and make a valued contribution
  to their community
- there is a shared commitment to action that considers the child's agency
  of voice and rights

DOI: 10.4324/9781003272526-9

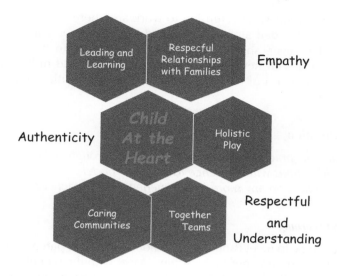

Figure 8.1 Person-centred early education practice (PEEP)

Working within a PCA setting has a commitment to team working, while simultaneously placing the child at the heart of their thinking. When individuals are open to continual learning and know how to implement a PCA into their practice change and development can occur.

- The practitioners consciously hold positive beliefs about their children and educate them as well as those working with them and beyond, including parents
- Practitioners focus on the individual's potential not their deficit
- Practitioners develop equal and ethical partnerships with the families of the children in their care
- Practitioners work and support the child as an individual in meeting their needs
- A PCA is developed and included within organisational structures and processes, such as supervision and parent partnerships
- A 'person centred culture' is promoted whereby behaviours, language as well as systems and processes are person-centred (Fig. 8.1).

Picture Portrait 1

Context

Pandora began nursery at seven months of age. She has two parents who both work with one returning from maternity leave. Pandora started nursery because her parents were returning to work and there was a little alternative. She had attended singing clubs and sensory clubs with her mother previously. However, she had not been separated from her mother and only met others with her. She has recently been offered milk in a bottle, with the introduction of food, as well as continuing with being breastfed in the evening.

Focused Question

How could the practitioners support Pandora through a PCA? Below are some considerations with reference to the PCA model.
    Can you reflect on any more from experience and practice?

Leading and Learning

Try to create time to meet Pandora in her home with both parents and encourage the parents to bring her to the setting. Meet with the parents regularly to share communication about the care of Pandora as well as her progress. As a practitioner, reflect on any challenges about her care and communicate these to senior staff, or the parent about how these could be positively resolved. This may be what type of bottle and teat Pandora prefers. Is she not taking much milk during the day?

Holistic Play

Accept Pandora as she is and aim to find what she likes to play with as an individual. Think about starting where she is not where they think she should be. In group care, it is easy to assume that all children of about X months enjoy X so do not be too quick to make these assumptions. Also, create opportunities such as nappy time to talk to her and create special qualitative moments to listen to Pandora. Observe Pandora as you meet her care needs when she cries and reflect on how she cries. Offer her support and try to find out what she is communicating through her cries.

Together Teams

As a team be honest about caring for a new infant with more senior staff, discussing settling in times with colleagues before she comes. Try to reflect on how you feel as a practitioner meeting and caring for a new infant. Being daunted or apprehensive is not unusual and certainly not considered unprofessional, although sometimes it is assumed the practitioner will be 'fine'.
    Compassion can be defined as 'a sensitivity to suffering in self and others with a commitment to try to alleviate and prevent it' (Gilbert et al., 2017: 46).
    'Conceptualize and analyse compassion as a collective activity comprising the acts of helping, including, comforting, and sharing, in the everyday life

of a kindergarten. These acts of compassion are dynamic, being negotiated, constituted, and produced in interaction' (Lipponen, 2018: 2).

Listen to each other and work together to find opportunities for Pandora to stay for a short time with a gradual increase as she settles in in an unhurried manner.

Respectful Relationships with Families and Caring Communities

Listen to Pandora is about mothers' concerns, choices and care about Pandora. Invite other members of the family as well as grandparents to the setting to meet the team in creating a whole community approach.

Picture Portrait 2

Context

Pete is a new member of staff; he recently qualified as a practitioner and can support and lead a small group of children. He is quite anxious about starting somewhere new and has only had the experience of placement practice. Below are some considerations with reference to the PCA model.

Focused Question

How could the practitioners support Pete through a PCA? Below are some considerations with reference to the PCA model.

Can you reflect on any more from experience and practice?

Leading and Learning

Create time to meet Pete and this is where supervision is a valuable part of the community's well-being. By meeting Pete regularly, a relationship can be developed, and training opportunities identified and offered. It is also helpful for Pete to recognise and appreciate the setting's ethos and philosophy. What type of setting is it? What play opportunities are offered? Why is this important to practice. Does Pete have time to read the setting policies to appreciate how this is put into practice?

It helps the process of becoming aware of self in relation to others and the universe. It brings unity and interconnectedness. (Bruce, 2020, n.p.).

Holistic Play

Pete may have been trained in a particular play pedagogy or philosophy. By finding out Pete's play philosophy, this can be nurtured and shared with the team at the setting. Does his thinking align or challenge the setting's approaches? How can these comfortable or even uncomfortable conversations be shared and negotiated? Often new practitioners bring new innovative ideas, a fresh lens to practice and this can be beneficial and challenging to those delivering familiar practices. Through authentic conversations, practices can grow and be nurtured, with the well-being of the children at the heart of practice.

Together Teams

Working together at staff meetings, training and buddy meetings can be valuable opportunities for staff to share practice. By giving Pete some autonomy and leading an aspect of practice demonstrates that he is being listened to and supported. If Pete himself is feeling anxious or concerned about an aspect of his role, the team can empathise reflecting on when they started and offering some advice.

Respectful Relationships with Families and Caring Communities

Pete's role as a practitioner may include being given specific roles. He may feel comfortable with some less and less with others. By listening and respecting how the roles can be delivered, Pete is able to fulfil his job. He may also be working times that result in seeing the parents less. By creating opportunities for him to meet the families and introduce himself to them, he is being welcomed in the setting with respect and value.

Picture Portrait 3

Context

Jess is a leader and would like to implement some thinking around the outdoors more. The setting has a large green area and a wooden area, but little is being done in it and she would like to create a growing area and begin to include topics around climate change. Although the teams are keen to get on board with the ideas, they are unsure where to begin and are having difficulty to see how they can connect it to the childcare they offer in meaningful ways. Below are some considerations with reference to the PCA model, with the contents developed by an UG student (Drinkall, 2022).

Focused Question

How could the practitioners support Jess through a PCA? Below are some considerations with reference to the PCA model.

Can you reflect on any more from experience and practice?

Leading and Learning

Children are encouraged to be able to explore the outdoors freely, developing their gross motor skills such as running, jumping as well as their confidence and self-belief which can directly link to mental health, well-being and self-esteem. Having the opportunity to play outdoors enables the children to learn about the world around them.

'*A lack of confidence and competence in performing these skills can have detrimental effects on children's social and emotional wellbeing*' (Evangelou, 2009: 72 in Archer and Siraj, 2015).

In developing this further, Jess also wanted to consider environmental sustainability in the setting community. This is defined as

'The responsibility to conserve natural resources and protect global eco-systems to support health and wellbeing now and in the future'.

She felt this could be challenging when trying to explain the concepts about environmental sustainability, including climate change to young children. Therefore, she thought that by beginning with the important themes of care and respect for the environment around them would be a good starting point. By encouraging exploration and experimenting with what they find outdoors such as leaves, stones, acorns, encourage discussion of this also. 'When children intuitively know that they are part of nature and it is part of them, with little sense of separation from it, they feel at home in the outdoors, can be nurtured by nature, and experience a need to care for and protect it throughout their lives' (Early Childhood Outdoors, 2021, n.p.).

Holistic Play

Jess wanted it to link to the Enabling Environments principle of the early year's curriculum connecting when a child feels emotionally safe and secure in an environment, they will be able to comfortably explore, touch, manoeuvre around their surroundings (DfE, 2021). Children could also make sense of their physical world and use their experiences to increase their knowledge of their environment (Department for Education, 2021). Therefore, the knowledge of sustainability and its importance can be linked to curriculum areas in meaningful ways with the children and the practitioners in developing their ideas too.

Together Teams

By supporting and working together, creating a strong and supportive team is vital as it ensures all practitioners can gain knowledge, support and encouragement in a setting. It is important for practitioners to carefully choose what resources they use in practice to make sure they are being role models for the children in their care when discussing sustainability, such as using sustainable materials and promoting sustainable practices, choosing loose parts and items that can be used and reused and collected from nature, such as stones, leaves, or sticks or things made with recycled materials.

A loose parts approach is used to enable children to take control of their own play and learning by using everyday natural objects rather than conventional 'toys'. Simon Nicholson (2009, 2019) defined loose parts as all the things that fulfil an individual's curiosity. Loose part, therefore, allows children to explore and provoke their play in many ways. (For example, a twig could be used as a magic wand.)

Respectful Relationships with Families and Caring Communities

By sharing ideas about sustainability with the parents, there are opportunities to develop this further, and as discussed in Chapter 7, a parent can become an active member of the community, sharing his expertise in planting and sowing to growing food and sharing his knowledge with the practitioners in maintaining the outside area.

End Note

Practitioners who attend to the individual needs of each child enable an opportunity for the children themselves to be heard. The practitioner also encourages a holistic approach to learning that supports their personal, social and emotional development. By referring to the model, a PCA is viewed as an approach underpinned by theoretical thinking but also meaningful to practice in many ways. By providing a few examples, it is hoped that the PCA will be a source of information and inspiration to those working with children at a time when their emotional well-being, following the pandemic, has been challenged and compromised under unprecedented conditions during the past few years. Children's emotional wellbeing has always been at the heart of the practice, and in contemporary practice, this continues to be essential for all early years community members from children to parents and practitioners. A PCA is an opportunity to reflect, feel nurtured and thrive together as part of the early community they belong to.

References

Archer, C. and Siraj, I. (2015) *Making the Case for Physical Activity* (p. 72). London: Sage Publications Ltd. https://dx.doi.org/10.4135/9781473920439.

Bruce, T. (2020) *Educating Young Children: A Lifetime Journey into a Froebelian Approach: The Selected Work of Tina Bruce*. London: Routledge.

Department for Education. (2021) *Statutory Framework for the Early Years Foundation Stage*. Available at: https://assets.publishing.service.gov.uk/government/uploads/system/uploads/attachment_data/file/974907/EYFS_framework_-_March_2021.pdf (Accessed 8/11/2022).

DfE (2021) Development Matters in https://assets.publishing.service.gov.uk/government/uploads/system/uploads/attachment_data/file/1007446/6.7534_DfE_Development_Matters_Report_and_illustrations_web__2_.pdf (Accessed 02/09/2022).

Drinkall, S. (2022) Play and Sustainability. Conference Paper. University of Winchester. Unpublished paper (Accessed 11/12/2022).

Early Childhood Outdoors. (2021) *Sustainability Mindset – Challenging the Norm and Raising Questions on Pedagogy and Practice*. Available at: https://www.earlychildhoodoutdoors.org/sustainability-mindset-challenging-the-norm-and-raising-questions-on-pedagogy-and-practice/ (Accessed 2/11/2022).

Evangelou, M. (2009) in Archer, C., and Siraj, I. (2015). *Making the case for physical activity* (p. 72). London. Sage. Publications Ltd, https://dx.doi.org/10.4135/9781473920439.

Gilbert, P., Catarino, F., Duarte, C. et al. (2017) The Development of Compassionate Engagement and Action Scales for Self and Others. *Journal of Compassionate Health Care*, 4, 4. https://doi.org/10.1186/s40639-017-0033-3

Lipponen, L. (2018) Constituting Cultures of Compassion in Early Childhood Educational Settings. In S. Garvis and E. E. Ødegaard (Eds.), *Nordic Dialogues on Children and Families. Evolving Families*, no. 2. Abingdon, Oxon: Routledge.

Nicholson, S. (2009) *How NOT to Cheat Children: The Theory of Loose Parts. Landscape Architecture.* Available at https://media.kaboom.org/docs/documents/pdf/ip/Imagination-Playground-Theory-of-Loose-Parts-Simon-Nicholson.pdf (Accessed 14/11/2022).

Nicholson, S. (2019) *Getting to Grips with Loose Parts Play.* PACEY. Available at https://www.pacey.org.uk/news-and-views/pacey-blog/2019/march-2019/getting-to-grips-with-loose-parts-play (Accessed 11/12/2022).

Sphere. (2022) What Is Environmental Sustainability? https://sphera.com/glossary/what-is-environmental-sustainability/ (Accessed 13/12/2022).

Index

Note: Page number in *italics* denote figures.

For Product Safety Concerns and Information please contact our EU
representative GPSR@taylorandfrancis.com Taylor & Francis Verlag GmbH,
Kaufingerstraße 24, 80331 München, Germany

Printed and bound by CPI Group (UK) Ltd, Croydon, CR0 4YY
08/06/2025
01896986-0018